LIVING THROUGH A NIGHTMARE

A TRUE STORY

By

PATRICIA HALEY HALL

ISBN: 1-4140-7120-5 (e-book)
ISBN: 1-4140-7121-3 (Paperback)

This book is printed on acid free paper.

1st Books - rev. 02/11/04

CHAPTER 1

Tragedies don't happen to us, they just happen to other people, or so we thought until that dreadful October Saturday in 1976 when we were faced with one beyond belief. Then we realized only too well that they do, indeed, happen to anyone, at anytime and anywhere, with no warning whatsoever.

After twenty-two years of marriage to a terrific husband, and four lovely children who had their share of battles but nevertheless retained a deep affection for one another, life seemed pretty wonderful to me. We had a large, close-knit family who were together often, all in the best of health. My husband Bob held an excellent federal position as chief of the Market News Service in the National Marine Fisheries, a position he thoroughly enjoyed. After a long retirement while the children were growing up, I had recently returned to work as a secretary in a small engineering firm, not far from home, with the part-time hours that fit in comfortably with our family schedule. We lived in a new home in a pleasant neighborhood, convenient to everything, and all six of us were involved in an assortment of activities that kept us busy and content. Life was rich, full, and wonderful, and we were on top of the world.

My last personal loss had been thirty years earlier when my kindly father, a favorite with everyone, was suddenly taken from us. His early death, leaving my mother with a young family to raise, was a cruel blow to all of us, one from which I never thought we'd recover. Thanks to my spunky little mother, however, who showed a courage and determination beyond anything we dreamed possible, we all pulled through intact. Gradually our lives took an upward swing and we were blessed with thirty years of continuous good luck, marred only by the accidents and broken bones prevalent in a family of boys.

When things go so completely right for such a long period of time, I suppose it's easy to become smug and complacent and expect them to go on that way forever. That must have been true in our case. Certainly we were ill-prepared for that black October Saturday in 1976 when our world fell apart forever. Then we knew with dead certainty that our lives would never again be the same. Bobby, our beloved eldest at twenty-one, was critically injured by a massive piece of machinery at the garage where he worked and the temporary loss of oxygen put him into a deep and lasting coma. For over two years he tried hard to work his way back to us, fighting off one infection and setback after another. But it was too much for him; the damage had been too extensive. On Thanksgiving Day of 1978, twenty-five months to the day after his accident, he left us forever. We lost him to death as quickly as we had lost him to the coma. He was gone before they could call from the hospital to tell us he had taken a bad turn. Then abruptly we had to face what we had refused to face for so many long and agonizing months. Bobby was gone, and all the hope and prayers we had for the miracle we so desperately needed would now never be answered. Somehow we had to pick up the pieces and continue with our lives that had been put on hold for so long. But we found it wasn't easy. Whereas living with the coma had been difficult, we found living without hope to be devastating.

This is the story of Bobby's brief life and of the long and heartbreaking months leading up to his untimely death.

PATRICIA HALEY HALL

CHAPTER 2

That black October Saturday returns forever to haunt me, as clear in my mind as if it had happened yesterday and yet seeming a century ago. And the weekend had started off so beautifully. Friday dawned bright and pleasant, a little cool. By noontime, however, it had turned into a beautiful Indian-summer-type day, pleasant for the end of October.

In mid-afternoon Brian, our second son, came bounding up the stairs with a big grin, happy to be home from college for the weekend and full of news about school, my mother, and other members of the family he had seen during the week. In college only a month, he attended the university in my hometown of Lowell, Massachusetts, a city about thirty miles north of Boston. During the week he lived with my mother and he commuted to our home in Peabody, on the north shore of Massachusetts, for the weekends.

Being the first in the family to live away from home, we sorely missed him during the week, and all of us looked forward to Friday when we would once again be together as a family. Larry, our third son, was especially lonesome for his pal. With only eighteen months separating them in age, the two boys had always been close. They shared the same room, activities, and many of the same friends.

I knew how much Larry looked forward to Fridays when Brian would again be home. With Bobby so busy at college,, work, and with his girlfriend Pat, and Brian away at school, the only other sibling at home was nine-year old Jane, our only daughter. Although she and Larry got along well enough, she was hardly the companion a sixteen-year-old boy needed at that time. A little later Larry came home from high school and soon the two boys were jogging down the street to round up some friends for a quick game of basketball. They came home at suppertime, tired but happy.

We always ate our evening meals together as a family, sitting around the dining room table long after the meal was over as each child told about his or her day. We never wanted them to be able to say we didn't listen to them, and that is a statement I honestly don't believe they can make. Sometimes there were heated arguments if one or another of the children had a certain gripe, but for the most part it was fun, and it was always my favorite time of the day. On the night before the accident there were a lot of laughs as Brian told about his week in college and the rest of the children had their turns trying to catch Brian up on their latest activities.

Bobby was the first to leave the table. He and his girlfriend Pat were going to a concert in a nearby town that evening, and he was anxious to shower and get ready. Then Brian called some friends to make arrangements to go out for the evening. Larry went down the street again to round up friends for another game of basketball, while Jane and her friends played in the yard.

After the news was over and Jane and Larry were in bed, Bob and I sat down to watch the late movie while we waited for the boys to come home. It was a funny/sad movie about two sheriffs, one white and one black who started out as enemies and ended up as friends. Brian was the first to come home, around midnight, and he sat down to watch it with us. Bobby arrived a little later and he, too, sat down to watch the ending. It ended on a funny note and he let out a hearty laugh. He looked so handsome sitting there in brown sweater and pants, with his blond wavy hair. I remember remarking to Bob how lucky we were to have the two of them around that night, because we had seen so little of them lately. I was so happily content, not knowing of the horror awaiting us just around the corner.

Saturday morning Jane was the first to awaken. When I heard her running around I asked her to check with Bobby to see if he had to work that day. He did, and he moaned, "Jane, will you give me a backrub?" When I got up I saw her straddled on his back as she gave him a backrub and tried to get him motivated to get up for work. An hour later he ran down the back stairs, so healthy and energetic, and it was the last time he ever left our home.

CHAPTER 3

At about 2:15 that afternoon the phone rang and Brian answered it. It was Bobby. He said he would be home at 3:00 o'clock to help him fix his car. Bobby had found an old car for sale at the garage and Brian bought it to commute to college. However, it needed bodywork and he told Brian to go to the hardware store for some filler and he would be home to help him repair it.

Half an hour later I was just picking up the phone to call friends to confirm dinner plans for that evening when Brian came bursting through the door. He asked if the garage had called me. Puzzled I asked why they would be calling me. He said Bobby had been taken to the hospital in an ambulance. He and Jane were driving past the garage when they saw an ambulance pulling out of the driveway. He went in to inquire what had happened and found out it was, indeed, Bobby in that ambulance.

I yelled to Bob, who was upstairs, and he came running down. He called the garage and then we left for the hospital. All the way over there I kept guessing, "I wonder if it was his leg again. Maybe he broke his arm." Nothing more serious than that even entered my mind. Bob said nothing. He knew it was serious. When he called the garage they told him he'd better hurry right over to the hospital.

Months later, Bob told me what had happened when he was upstairs and I called him down. We live in such close proximity to several shopping centers and highways that the sound of a siren is an everyday occurrence. However, when Bob heard the siren that afternoon, he said he had such an eerie feeling and knew immediately that it was going to affect us. At the time I called him down, he was frantically trying to get the police on Bobby's scanner, but the aerial was broken and he couldn't receive anything on it.

When we got to Emergency, it was alive with activity, complete with the policemen. I thought that was the normal commotion there, never realizing all of it was being centered on Bobby, who was in a cubicle not far away. When we asked to see our son, they ushered us into a little room, and I thought they were going to see which patient was our son. But they knew.

The first idea I had of the seriousness of his injury was when Jane's Campfire leader, a nurse in Emergency, came into the room. Her usually pleasant face was somber as she put her arm around my shoulder and said, "Oh, Pat, I'm so sorry." Puzzled I asked, "Is he all right, Maryann?" She just shook her head sadly and said, "It's bad." OH, GOD, PLEASE NOT BOBBY!

A short time later a priest came in - new to our parish that week and one I had yet to meet. He introduced himself to us and then said he had anointed Bobby, the last rites for a Catholic before death. ANOINTED? HE WAS ON THE PHONE AN HOUR AGO! Everything was happening so fast, and all of it so dreadful, that I was having a hard time getting it to sink in.

Then a kindly doctor came in, the kindest professional we were to meet during our twenty-five months of hell. Looking directly at us he explained that when Bobby arrived his heart was like a bag of worms, but they had stabilized him. Bobby was now in a coma and he didn't know when, or if, he would come out of it. He explained that they were moving him to a hospital in the adjoining city of Salem, where they had an intensive care unit. Heartbroken, I asked if he had ever seen anyone that bad who had survived. His answer kept me going for months. He said he had been in a coma when he was twelve years old. Right there and then I decided that if he could make it, Bobby could make it.

The doctor then suggested we go home for a few hours while they moved Bobby, and then we could visit him after he was settled at Salem Hospital. When we got home the children met us at the door looking dazed and frightened. One look at our faces, and their worst fears were confirmed. Their safe little world had just crumbled. Bob explained what had happened, and then we had the difficult calls to the rest of the family.

Arriving at Salem Hospital we were met by two solemn-faced doctors who gave us little hope. They said they were taking Bobby down for an angiogram, an x-ray taken through a tiny tube inserted into the heart to see if there was any damage to his heart. Incredibly, his heart wasn't damaged. He didn't even have a broken rib or a mark on

11

his body. To have been crushed so severely without having broken bones was unusual.

After he was settled into his room we went in, and the sight of him made me want to die. His eyes were covered, he had tubes down his throat and nose, and there were electrical leads taped all over his chest that were attached to machines. I couldn't believe it was the same son who was so alive and happy such a few hours earlier. I was numb.

While we were there Bobby's girl Pat and her father came into the room. She and Bobby had a date for that evening, and she was shocked when Bob called to tell her what had happened.

We spent hours there that night, but could only visit him for a few minutes each hour. Suddenly we were surprised to see the bishop from our church come into the waiting room. He had just been elevated to bishop at the first of the month, and the following morning was having his final Mass and reception prior to leaving for his new assignment. The new priest we had met at the hospital was his replacement. The bishop spent about an hour with us that night and was such a comfort.

About midnight they advised us there was nothing we could do at the hospital, and that we should go home and sleep. SLEEP!! There was no sleep for us that evening. We just sat in the living room in a daze, afraid the phone would ring telling us he was gone. Every now and then Bob would call the hospital, only to be told that he was just the same.

In the morning Bob went over to the hospital while I waited for my sister Ruth and her husband Bill Quealy to bring my mother down. Always closest to the family member who needed her most at any given time, I knew Mother would want to be with Bobby, even though I thought the sight of him would frighten her. We visited him in the afternoon and evening, and at night my sister Gay and her husband Bob McEvoy came down to bring Mother home.

Monday morning we went to the hospital and at noon went to Mass at a nearby church. There I met an older woman who did filing in our office. I explained what had happened and turned in my key, asking her to tell my boss that I had to resign because I didn't know what was going to happen. That night he called and told me to take the time I needed, but not to resign. I was out for a week and then returned, because my office was right around the corner from the hospital. I knew I could be there faster from the office than from my home. That part-time job saved my sanity. It was just what I needed for a few hours each day to keep my mind off my troubles.

CHAPTER 4

On the Tuesday following the accident, Bob and Brian went down to the garage to see just what had happened. I didn't want to hear all the gory details, and to this day I have never read the official report. When they came home they gave me a brief description of what they were told.

The following weekend the garage was having a circus to promote the new 1977 cars. Bobby was scheduled to replace missing light bulbs around the place. He didn't have a license to operate heavy-duty equipment, but for some strange reason they had him drive a big payloader, climb into the bucket, and replace the fluorescent tubes in the lights. I don't know why they didn't have him use a stepladder. This was the old type payloader where the arms to the bucket ran along the side of the machine, instead of being up front as they now are.

When Bobby was getting back into the cab of the machine, after replacing a bulb, the bucket arms were suddenly activated and he was caught between the arm and the door of the machine. The machine jammed, and they couldn't get it up or down. The minutes he was crushed there without oxygen is what put him into the coma.

As I listened to Bob recount the accident, I watched Brian's face and it was twisted in agony. He snarled, "Why didn't they get him out of there on time?" Bob tried to explain that it was a huge piece of machinery and that it was defective. The veins stood out on Brian's neck as he clenched his fists and said, "But there were a lot of GUYS there!" The poor kid. I could almost see him trying to pull that machine off his brother single handedly if he had been at the garage minutes earlier. If ever I doubted our children loved each other, I never will again. No siblings could have ached over their brother more than our three did.

Wednesday noontime we went to Mass again and when we returned to the hospital they asked permission to operate on Bobby and give him a tracheotomy. For the previous days they had the tube that assisted him to breathe down his throat. However, if Bobby came out of the coma, the tube could have damaged his throat, so they wanted a permanent tracheotomy. He recovered from that operation very well.

From then on we had a regular routine to our lives, all worked around Bobby's visiting hours. I only worked until 1:00 p.m., so by 1:15 p.m. I would be at the hospital. Then I'd rush home to see Larry and Jane and to prepare supper. As soon as we finished eating, Bob and I would take off for the hospital again. If Larry was busy, Jane came with us. Night after night she patiently waited in the lounge doing her homework while we visited Bobby. I knew she wanted to go in, but she never nagged us about it. She was only nine at the time, and I thought the shock of seeing him like that would be too much for her. I never counted on her incredible faith and strength.

During the next week they gave Bobby another operation. This time they put a feeding tube into his stomach. Those two operations at least took the tubes out of his nose and throat, and he looked much better. However, the second operation eventually caused him trouble because of his weakened condition. That operation never healed from inside and they had to open him up to have it heal from within. For the next few months we had one setback after another until it finally healed.

Over and over again during those months I wondered what we had done that was so terrible we deserved this agony. We had always tried to live by the book and to bring the children up accordingly. We were never in a hurry for them to grow up and be on their way. Rather, we thoroughly enjoyed their youth. When I saw other parents who ran roughshod over everyone and everything in their way to get what they wanted and they seemed to have good luck, it hurt.

But then I thought of the wonderful people I knew who had suffered tragedies and realized that most people do not go through life without suffering heartache, and that I shouldn't question God's judgment.

CHAPTER 5

During those endless hours waiting in the outer office of Intensive Care, I tried to read, but it was useless because I couldn't concentrate on what I was reading. Then I tried knitting, but that, too, was hopeless. Finally I turned to what I liked to do the best - write. Fortunately I had never forgotten my shorthand, and I jotted down everything that was happening to us so we could tell Bobby about it when he came out of the coma.

My mind went back to the beautiful beginning of his life. He was born on Holy Thursday in April of 1955 when we were living in our first home in Lowell. Blond, blue-eyed and beautiful, and in perfect health, he was everything anyone could ever ask for in a child and, like most new parents, we were elated.

Bob and I met during the Korean War when I was working as a civilian secretary at Fort Devens Army Hospital and he, in the army at the time, was assigned to the hospital personnel office. I commuted to the fort daily from my home in Lowell, Massachusetts. Once an old mill city famous for

PATRICIA HALEY HALL

its "mile of mills" along the banks of the Merrimack River, by 1976 it had become a thriving community. It boasted an excellent university, three major hospitals, a popular national park and, good for the economy of the city, was the headquarters for the giant Wang computer industry.

Bob, on the other hand, was born and raised in the westernmost part of the state, not far from the New York border. His town of Stockbridge was a quaint little community nestled deep in the valleys of the Berkshire Mountains. A town rich in history, it became better known in recent years as the home of Norman Rockwell, America's most beloved illustrator. Rockwell, who lived next door to Bob's brother Ernest, featured Ernest, Bob's father, and other members of the family on his covers over the years.

By the time the war ended, Bob and I were engaged and he was faced with the decision of whether or not to return to Stockbridge to begin his career, or settling closer to Boston where he thought his chances might be greater. Lucky for me, he took a civil service exam and was assigned to the Boston office of the National Marine Fisheries. It was the beginning of a long, pleasant, and successful career. He bought a small home in Lowell and the following year we were married, settling down to what we thought would be a lifetime of living among our family and friends.

Although I loved office work and felt I had a good chance of advancing in my position, when Bobby came along the following year we both knew we wanted him to have a full-time mother. It was a decision I have never regretted making, most especially since we lost him so early in life.

As it turned out, I couldn't have worked had I wanted to. In the first five years of our marriage we moved from office to office so that Bob could advance in his position. Those years took us to New York, Chicago, Baltimore, and then back to Boston. We bought and sold a couple of more homes along the way. It was a hectic, but pleasant time of our lives.

While we were in New York we lived on Staten Island and Bob commuted to Manhattan daily via the ferry. At the end of our first year in New York, he came down with a recurrence of the rheumatic fever he had had as a child. The doctor told him it was caused by dampness, evidently from the time he spent on the water in the ferry, and advised him to stay out of damp places. After that warning, we were anxious to return to Boston to eliminate the daily ferry rides. However, that transfer seemed remote, so we resigned ourselves to staying in New York and bought a home on the island, moving in two weeks before our second son, Brian, was born.

When Brian was a few months old, Bob received a call from the Washington office telling him the assistant director of the Boston office had abruptly resigned to accept a position in another agency. Our prayers were answered and Bob was quick to apply for the Boston position. We moved back to Massachusetts the day Brian turned six months old. This time, in an effort to omit the long commute from Lowell, we bought a home in the Boston suburb of Somerville, and there we spent the thirteen most pleasant years of our lives.

CHAPTER 6

Our third son, Larry, was born the following year and we settled down into the usual activities involved with raising a young family. The children were enrolled in the Catholic school and soon, because I "didn't work", Bobby was volunteering me for every field trip and activity that came along. I once complained that if I visited the Museum of Science ONE MORE TIME they'd make me one of their exhibits. Bob just laughed and said, "You know you're flattered that your son wants you with him." And I was.

Soon both Bob and I were involved in a number of activities at the school, church, scouts and clubs. The church had a very active men's club, and Bob soon was elected vice-president and then president. There were many social activities there, and it was an exciting time of our lives. The men's club consisted of an assortment of men of different ages, professions, and nationalities, and yet they worked well together and did a lot for the church. Although we had moved from Somerville six years before Bobby's death, all the men showed up at his wake. A month later they paid us the ultimate tribute by contributing their annual scholarships in Bobby's name. From then on a plaque bearing his name was hung in the school corridor, alongside his picture, and the names of the boy and girl winners of the graduating class were added each year.

I thought about returning to work on a part-time basis when Larry started school, but my plans were foiled with the arrival of Jane, our only daughter. Bobby was twelve when she was born and I thought he'd be unhappy at the thought of having a little sister around. Quite the opposite was true. From the time he first spotted her in the hospital, she was his little pet. It was as if she had two fathers - both wrapped securely around her little finger.

He was very good to her and when he went to the fairs would always promise to win her a stuffed animal. And he did. One year he took a girl to a fair and the first animal he won was tucked under his arm for Jane. Only after he won a second time did the girl he was with receive her animal. I often wondered what she thought of that arrangement.

Bobby had a small bowl on his desk in which he put his change every night. He told Jane she could have whatever he put in there. One day I was taking her to the bank with a sizable deposit. He asked where she got the money and when she told him it was his change from the desk, he told her from then on to only take the pennies. I guess he thought that money would look better in his bank account than in her's.

Just a few weeks before his fatal accident he and Pat had told Jane they would take her horseback riding on a Sunday afternoon. Then Pat realized she had a bridal shower to attend, so Bobby said they would take her the following week. Jane was spoiled by him and nagged that he had promised to take her. I told him to just ignore her and go on with whatever he wanted to do, but he broke down and took her riding.

By the time they got there only one horse was available, so Jane rode the horse for the next hour while Bobby ran beside her through the muddy fields. Not many young fellows would do that for their sisters . But all the love he showered on her during her nine years with him was repaid by her strong faith and courage during his illness. I don't think many nine year olds could have done as much. She was an inspiration to all of us, and I knew then why she was sent to us so late in life.

One time I was really down and she admonished me that God was testing us like He did Abraham on the mountain with his son, and that I had to have faith that Bobby would make it. At the time I wondered which one of us was the mother and which one the child.

PATRICIA HALEY HALL

CHAPTER 7

Bobby was always a very independent little guy. When we moved to Somerville he was about ready to enter kindergarten. There were several boys his age in the neighborhood, which made it nice. However, their friendships were already established and it was a little hard for him to break into their group. That didn't really bother him. He seemed to march to his own drummer. Whenever that happened, he'd just come home and get busy setting something up on his own. One time it was a carnival in the garage. He blew up balloons, taped them to a large board, and put pins on sticks to throw at them. He also blocked off another board for a penny toss. He seemed to come up with some creative games and soon everyone in the neighborhood wanted to join in.

Another time he got out his wagon, put on the covered wagon canvas he had received for Christmas, got his brothers together and took a lunch and drinks for a trip around the block. In no time at all, the other neighborhood children got their wagons out and joined them. They had a lot of fun in that neighborhood.

Bob bought them a motor boat and they all loved it. We vacationed at the large lakes in New Hampshire where Bobby, especially, loved running around the lake and taking the others water skiing. He was so proud of that boat and was always buying something or other to fix it up. We still feel it was one of the best purchases we ever made because it brought the family so much pleasure.

Bobby never thought of himself as last when he could think of himself as first. One story we still laugh about today happened when he was about thirteen years old. It was a custom in our church to have a May procession on a Sunday in May where the members of the various church organizations marched in a solemn procession through the streets surrounding the church. A statue of the Blessed Virgin Mary would be carried on a pedestal leading the procession. At the end of the march we all entered the church for Benediction and the crowning of Mary. One of the girls in the graduation class was chosen to put the crown of flowers on Mary.

All of us were scheduled to be in the procession. Bob, as president of the Men's Club was going to march with his group carrying the statue of Mary. I was treasurer of the Ladies' Sodality and was supposed to march with the women. However, Jane was still in the carriage so I chose, instead, to watch from the sidelines. All three boys were marching with the altar boys.

Three days earlier Bobby came in and announced that he was going to lead the first communicants, a group of second graders who had made their first communion the previous Saturday. A few minutes later Brian came in and said Bobby was the tallest altar boy so he had to be last in line. Puzzled I said, "I thought you were going to lead the first communicants." Undaunted, he just said, "I am," and I let it go at that conversation.

On Sunday afternoon I stood watching as the procession proceeded. First Bob went by with his group, then Brian and Larry came along with the altar boys. The last altar boy passed by and I had all I could do not to laugh out loud during all that solemnity. Leaving a wide distance between the last altar boy and himself, Bobby marched like a priest leading his flock in front of the next group in line - the first communicants. Never be last when you can think of yourself as first seemed to be his motto. It is memories like that that keep him alive to us today.

CHAPTER 8

The day before Bobby entered third grade the boys were playing in the yard with a big box that came from someone's new television. They put blankets in the bottom and then jumped off the back deck into the box. When that collapsed, they laid it along our driveway, which went downhill, and ran and slid on the box.

All day long they seemed to be yelling "Mother" and I'd go out to settle one dispute or another. Around suppertime I told them I was busy and wasn't coming out again. When Bobby again yelled for me, I told him to come in. He came crawling in the front door and said he had hurt his leg. I felt terrible. When he slid on the box his leg buckled under him and it broke. Bob came in just about then and took him to the doctor. He came home a little later wearing a cast.

He broke the same leg again when he was a sophomore in high school. When he ran out the back door he slid on some ice and fell. He was wearing high cowboy boots at the time and the doctor said if he had shoes on, it probably wouldn't have broken. I had to cut his pants along the seam and put wedges in them to accommodate the cast.

One morning he called from high school. He was walking down the steps when he banged the cast on one of the steps, causing it to break. I took him to the hospital and they put another cast right over the previous one. It must have been terribly heavy, but he maneuvered those crutches like a pro and never complained. Broken bones are something you have to expect when you have boys, I suppose.

The only other problem he had during his brief life was a bout of pneumonia. At the end of his third grade we had gone to Stockbridge for Memorial Day weekend. We stayed with Bob's parents while Bobby stayed at his Uncle Ernest's house to be with his cousin Michael. On Monday morning we went up to Ernest's and while the other children were playing in the yard, Bobby was resting on the couch. That was unusual for him, but Ernest said he didn't seem to be feeling well.

We went to the parade in town and shortly after that left for home. Tuesday morning he didn't feel well so I kept him home from school. He felt better later in the morning and insisted on going for the afternoon session. Wednesday was a repeat of Tuesday. He stayed home in the morning but wanted to go in the afternoon.

At suppertime I mentioned it to Bob and he said he didn't like the looks of him because his lips seemed a little blue, so he took him to the doctor. Sure enough, he had pneumonia and the doctor put him into the hospital. He was there for ten days and it took us ten weeks for him to get a clear x-ray.

Those weeks were terrible for me. My nerves were so on edge. One night the principal of Bobby's school called and said one of the nuns was transferring to another school and had to be in Portsmouth, New Hampshire early the next morning. Some of the other nuns were going up there with her because they were having a little reception for her prior to her leaving for her new assignment.

The woman who planned on taking them to New Hampshire had car trouble. They knew we had a station wagon and asked if we could possibly accommodate them. We would be staying most of the day while the nuns had their reception, so they suggested I pack a picnic lunch.

The nuns were left a beautiful little island by a rich New York lawyer. It had several buildings on it and a large, beautiful home. I packed the lunch and a blanket and when we got there they showed us around, told us where the rest rooms were, and got on with their party.

That day was wonderful for me, after all those tense weeks while Bobby was ill. It was so relaxing on that beautiful island right off the New Hampshire coast. Bobby rested on the blanket while the boys and I picked up shells, and played along the shore, and then we had our picnic. It was just what I needed at that time. When we got home the nuns thanked me for taking them, but I felt they were the ones who deserved the thanks. I needed to get away from home that day and the fresh air and sunshine seemed to do wonders for Bobby. Shortly after that, he was completely cured.

PATRICIA HALEY HALL

CHAPTER 9

You could set your clock by Bobby's return from school, always at the same time. One day when he was eight years old, the other boys came in, but still no Bobby. Some friends of his had joined cub scouts a few weeks earlier and I had a hunch that was where he was. When he came home he said he had signed up for scouts and that they were having a pack meet that Friday. He had to bring in a pet and tell something about it, what it ate and how he cared for it. We didn't have any pets so Bob went out and bought a turtle and food for his project.

At the meeting I went up to his new den mother and thanked her for taking him in. She said she already had a big enough den but that Bobby was such a polite little boy she hated to refuse him. Later they called for volunteer den mothers. I thought that if that woman, with eight children of her own, could run a den then the least I could do was volunteer. That was the beginning of four busy years working with those young boys. Bob also got involved in it by becoming chairman.

The den mothers each did what they liked the best. One was our treasurer, one ran all the field trips, one ran the blue and gold banquet, as well as set up food for the pack meets. I ran the monthly pack meets. I knew many of the boys would never have a chance to be on stage, so each month I planned a skit so that they could perform for their parents, and the boys loved it. At Christmas time I made Santa and reindeer costumes for their skit and Indian and other costumes for their performances. Whenever I needed a master of ceremonies, I always drafted Bobby for the job. He enjoyed it, and would ad lib as he went along. That led to his joining the drama club in high school.

When Bobby was eleven years old, the director of the foreign fisheries called from Washington asking Bob to take the position of fishery attache working out of the U.S. Embassy in Abidjan, on the Ivory Coast of Africa. It was a prestigious position, one that doesn't come along very often, and he was pleased to accept. We prepared to put our house up for sale and told Bobby he could tell his friends he was moving to Africa. We were also scheduled to go to Washington for a quick course in French, the language in Abidjan.

The State Department's report arrived detailing the living conditions in Abidjan, however, and after reading it Bob was forced to withdraw his acceptance. It said the area was very damp with a long rainy season, just what the doctor on Staten Island had told him to avoid after his bout with rheumatic fever. Bobby was especially disappointed when Bob withdrew his acceptance. He believed his friends would think he was lying, but he wasn't. We honestly thought we'd be leaving Somerville. He was uprooted so often in his early years that he was restless and always ready to go on to a new adventure. It is strange that his last journey was taken far earlier than the rest of us.

Bobby attended high school at St. Mary's in Cambridge and as a member of the drama society he appeared in their annual shows each of the three years he spent there. In his sophomore year they presented "THE SOUND OF MUSIC" and he played the part of Rolph, the messenger boy. He sang "YOU ARE SIXTEEN GOING ON SEVENTEEN" and he was great. Never one to sing around the house, we were unaware he had such a fine voice. We were beaming at his performance and many people came up to us later to say he had a beautiful voice. Bob and I were so proud. Even though it was a snowy night, as usual the family came down from Lowell to see him, and they were equally proud.

For Christmas that year we had bought him a tape recorder and Bob planned on taping the show to give to him with his gifts on Christmas morning. As luck would have it, the machine was defective and we never got the tape. How I wish I had had him tape it on the new recorder after Christmas, but he didn't want to sing at home. After his death I wrote to the principal and others, trying to get a copy of that tape, but none could be found. It would be priceless to me now that he's gone.

Bobby and two others in the show were invited to tour with a popular singing group that summer, but try as we did to convince him to accept the invitation, he adamantly refused. That surprised us, because he was always the one looking for a change. I often wonder what his life would have been, had he accepted that opportunity.

CHAPTER 10

At the end of Bobby's junior year of high school, Bob was transferred to the regional office in Gloucester, on the far north shore of Massachusetts. We decided to move to the city of Peabody, an equal distance from Gloucester, my family in Lowell, and our friends in Somerville. This time the boys said they wanted to go to the public schools, so Bobby spent his senior year at Peabody High School where he was instrumental in starting a photography club, becoming its first president. At the end of the year he enrolled at our local college.

In college Bobby started out studying business administration, but the following year changed to law enforcement. At the same time he took the civil service exam for policemen and received an excellent score. At that time, however, they were only hiring minorities and female police, so I knew his chances of receiving an appointment were slim.

Between his sophomore and junior years of college he went out one morning, all dressed up in a sport coat and tie, looking for a summer job. At noon he came home and was quite discouraged. No one had hired him. He said he should have worn jeans and a tee shirt so they'd think he needed a job. I told him not to be discouraged, that his father had never pressured him to get a job, and that something would come up eventually.

That afternoon he received offers for three positions, two of which he accepted. One was at the garage; the other was as a part-time salesman in a cigar store a few evenings a week. Little did we realize that garage job would cost him his life.

When school began in September he dropped the part-time position and decided to attend evening college. We tried to talk him into continuing his schooling during the day so he could get his degree that much sooner. Bob even offered to pay him a salary to keep him going days. However, he was independent and determined to do it his way. He found the night classes more interesting because they were small, were taught by professional law employees who worked during the day, and that at night he was a name and not just a number.

Bobby was never one who dreamed of making a million dollars. His idea of a wonderful life was to be a policeman or sheriff in some small New Hampshire town where he could have a home and family and enjoy his boat and his skiing, but even that was denied him.

He and Pat loved to ski, play tennis, ride his boat, water ski and ride their bikes - all the nice things you want your children to do. They had a great time together, and I was thankful the last few years of his life were so happy. I just wish he could have had the time to prove what he could have accomplished in his life.

PATRICIA HALEY HALL

CHAPTER 11

In May of 1976, five months before the accident, I called my friend Germaine Robillard in Somerville. She always answered the phone in such an upbeat manner, so I was surprised to hear a hollow "hello". When I asked what was the matter, she said her son Eddie, a friend of Brian's, had been in an automobile accident the previous night and was critical in the intensive care unit at a local hospital.

A few days later I drove her to the hospital and waited in the lobby while she went in to see her son. As I sat there I watched the agonized faces of the families as they left the rooms of their critically ill relatives. I remember thinking, "I could never bear it if one of my family ended up critically ill." Little did I realize that, five months later, we would be facing something infinitely worse. It's good we don't know what's ahead for us, or I don't think we could handle it.

After he died I wondered if Bobby had a premonition of his death. When he and Pat spent the day skiing it was very expensive and I mentioned to him that he used to be so careful saving his money and that now he was spending it like mad. He surprised me by saying, "Pat and I were talking about that and we said we don't know how long we'll be here so we might as well do what we want while we can." That surprised me coming from one so young.

Then again he startled me by saying, "Mother, if anything ever happened to me I'd want to donate my eyes to some blind person so that they could see." I was horrified and said, "Bobby, don't even THINK of that." At the time he died I was so distraut I never gave it a thought. In retrospect, however, I wish we had. I'd like to believe that at least part of him was alive today, but it is too late to go back. I admire people I hear about now who are thoughtful enough in their grief to help other people. I know if one of my family needed a transplant I would be willing to beg anyone and everyone who could be of help.

One night we arrived at Salem Hospital but couldn't get in to see Bobby because they had a "Code 9". When I inquired at the desk the receptionist was so upset. She said they had just brought a fellow in on an overdose - for the third time - and they were working on him. She said it made her furious when she saw how hard Bobby was working to recover and that fellow was trying to kill himself. I felt the same way.

CHAPTER 12

The months following Bobby's accident were a nightmare as he had one setback after another. By the time Thanksgiving day arrived, he had been in the coma for a month and Jane had yet to see him. Although everyone in the family had invited Mother to Thanksgiving dinner, I knew she only wanted to be with Bobby that day. She insisted on cooking the entire meal herself, and my brother, Fred Haley, drove her down to save me the trip.

That morning the boys went to the football game so Bob said he was going to take Jane over to see Bobby while I waited for Mother to arrive. They came home at noontime and Bob was shaking his head in disbelief. He said, "We don't have to worry about that little girl. She has her head squarely on her shoulders."

Although the last time she had seen Bobby was the morning of the accident when he kissed her good-bye and went running down the steps with a lively gait, she never hesitated a minute when she entered his room. Bob said she went right to the stool beside his bed, stood on it and

45

reached over to kiss him. Then, for the rest of the morning, she held his hand and told him everything that had happened during the month. For the rest of the morning she proceeded to describe the Macy Thanksgiving day parade as it passed by on the television screen. From then on we never kept anything from her. She was with us to the end.

Shortly before Christmas I went straight from work to Jane's school where they were having a class display on Egypt. As soon as I finished there, I went to the hospital where I found that Bobby had suffered a seizure and had stopped breathing altogether. They had been trying to wean him off the respirator and had cut down on the assists he was getting every minute. I don't know if they cut back too quickly, or what it was, but he had to be put back on full respiration again. My heart hit rock bottom.

A few minutes later Bob arrived from work. The doctors had called him as soon as it had happened. Right in front of Bobby the doctor explained how critical he was. Bob hit the roof. He ushered the doctor out of the room and told him in no uncertain terms that he never wanted him to talk like that in the room with Bobby. No one knew what he could or couldn't hear, and we didn't want him frightened any more than he probably already was. They agreed in our presence, but we don't know what happened when we weren't there.

A few days later we went to Mass on Christmas eve, my favorite night of the year. That year, however, even the sight of the beautiful church with the red poinsettias against the white marble altar and the stirring music did little to lift my spirits. I couldn't help but sob all the way through Mass. He was so sick. Jane just smiled and whispered, "Everything will be all right." She had such faith.

PATRICIA HALEY HALL

CHAPTER 13

Fortunately I never required much sleep because there was little to be had during our twenty-five months living with the coma. There was so much to do and so little time in which to do it that we seemed to be constantly on the go. I think we were working on our nerves, and knew we needed to keep busy as a diversion from the tragedy we were facing.

From the day of the accident I felt like someone had pushed me into a hole and the harder I tried to get out of it the further I was pushed. It was such a weird feeling. I almost didn't want to get up in the morning because I didn't know what was ahead for me.

Mornings had always been my best time of the day. I could get a day's work finished in a few hours before going to work. After the accident I went faster than ever, but I still seemed to be dragging myself. It was like one "me" was living through the misery while another "me" was watching from the sidelines. Unconsciously I must have been hoping I would wake up and find it was just a bad dream.

It was somehow bearable when others were around, but the alone times were difficult. Nights when the others were asleep I would lay awake trying to feel what Bobby was feeling, wondering if he could hear us and if he was frightened.

Over and over again I had the same nightmare. I was beside Bobby's bed when he started falling. As I reached to grab him he kept falling out of my grasp. I'd wake up in a cold sweat and there was no more sleep for me that night.

We also had several middle-of-the-night phone calls during that time. I don't know if they were legitimate wrong numbers, or if some sick person was getting his jollies by calling us up at that hour. I do know that I would freeze when the phone rang and would stay that way until Bob came back to tell me who it was. When I think of all that happened during those twenty-five months, I marvel we came through it as well as we did.

CHAPTER 14

So many unbelievable things happened to us during our years of hell, things that never happened before and we doubt will ever happen again. And many of them had nothing to do with Bobby.

I suppose the most bizarre of all would have to be the night Bob and I were caught in the middle of a shootout. In early January of 1977, three months into the coma, we were returning from the hospital a little later than usual because Bobby had another bad turn. As we approached the monument where we turned left heading to Peabody, I was lost in my own sad thoughts and only vaguely noticed a police cruiser turning into the road in front of us. My attention perked up, however, when the police pulled to the left side of the road in the face of approaching traffic.

Fully expecting the police to cross back in front of us, Bob almost slowed the car to a halt. Suddenly the cruiser stopped nose-to-nose with an oncoming car, which was followed by a third (unmarked police) car. We watched in horror as the occupants of all three vehicles jumped out wielding guns. The operator of the middle automobile was in direct line of fire with our windshield.

Bob was the first to react. Shouting, "Duck, it's a shootout," he pushed my head down under the dashboard and leaned over on top of me. We heard bullets flying all around us and then I glanced up to see a detective running by the car carrying a rifle. A few minutes later he returned, this time carrying two weapons. Inching his head up over the dashboard, Bob shouted, "They got him. He's over there in a snow bank." After that, the police came over and waved us out of there and issued orders to seal off the area. As we drove by the cruiser, I noticed it riddled with bullets. We were both shaking and stopped down the street where Bob got out to check our car. Fortunately, none of the bullets had found their way to us.

When we arrived home, our troubles with Bobby were temporarily set aside as we recounted the shootout with Larry and Jane. The minute the words were out of my mouth I could have bitten my tongue. They both turned white. They had lived through so much misery over the past three months without complaining. Now they thought they had almost lost their parents in a gunfight. How I wish I had made light of the incident, but it was too late for that. How much more heartache were they going to have to face?

That evening the news reported that the man they shot was a nineteen-year old Salem man who was suspected of stabbing his five-year old niece to death in New Hampshire the previous day. He was shot in the neck and taken to Salem Hospital.

When I arrived at the hospital the next day, I told the receptionist about the shooting and she said he was right in there next to Bobby. Sure enough, he was there complete with a police guard. A few days later he was recovered and on his way out of the hospital, ready to face trial. Meanwhile, my poor son, who had done nothing wrong, was still in the hospital, unable to awaken. It seemed so unfair.

That afternoon our local paper reported that the nineteen year old Salem man had been babysitting his five year old niece in New Hampshire the previous day. The little girl was found dead in her parent's basement apartment and the uncle was missing. She had been stabbed in the back. Rifles were stolen from the home of the little girl's parents and the uncle was being charged with her death. He had suffered a gunshot wound in his encounter with the police.

PATRICIA HALEY HALL

CHAPTER 15

In mid-January I was visiting Bobby when the nurse called me into the middle of the intensive care unit to answer the telephone. I knew that inner sanctum was off-limits to all but hospital personnel, so I was surprised when they had me take the call there instead of at the receptionist's desk. My knees were shaking by the time I reached the phone. It was Larry and he was a wreck.

Brian had called him from Lowell telling him he had been hit broadside by a woman driver and the car was totaled. Fortunately Brian wasn't hurt, but Larry was terribly upset.

We called Brian that night and he said he was stopped in traffic when a driver on the other side of the road tried to stop, but skidded right across the road to his car. The driver's side was completely demolished. He noticed her coming, so he leaned over in the seat to get out of the way, which saved him from serious injury.

When we saw the car later in the week I was sick. He could so easily have been hurt badly in an accident like that. We were grateful he had Bob's old Buick, which was built like a tank, instead of the old car he had bought at the garage.

The following month we had just returned from the hospital and I was in the kitchen making a Betsy Ross costume for Jane's school project when the phone rang. It was my brother Fred. The minute I heard his voice I braced for more trouble - and it came. My mother was in here store that afternoon when a teenager came in and robbed her. Even at our advanced ages we never crossed my mother, so the thought of some young punk demanding her hard-earned money infuriated her and she demanded he leave the store. Instead, he knocked her down. She fell back into the kitchen, banging her shoulder on the stove as she slipped unconscious to the floor. That little thief stole the money and left her there, not caring whether she was alive or dead.

Mother awoke almost immediately and phoned the police. When they arrived they saw she was hurting but she refused to go to the hospital. When she mentioned my nephew Jim Quealy was a member of the Lowell Rescue Squad, they called him and he rushed right over. Jim was more than a grandson, he was like another son. He lived near Mother and was always dropping by to see what he could do for her. He talked her into going to the hospital with him, but she refused to be admitted. She had a very painful dislocated shoulder. They kept her in Emergency until later that night and most of the family showed up. Fred called only after they had her home in her own bed. No one wanted to call us with more bad news.

The robber went up to the park and bragged about knocking off the store. All the kids in the neighborhood liked my mother, so they reported him to a mailman who was going by. He recognized the thief as one of his neighbors over by the college, and before midnight the police had called Jim to tell him they had the robber in custody. That brat will never know how lucky he was that the police got to him before my brother Fred did. Fred was only twenty when my father died. The only boy in the family, he took seriously his position as man of the family. He was willing to take on anyone, no matter their size, if they were a threat to any one of us.

The following day Fred went over to the home of the boy and demanded to see his brother, who was with him at the time of the robbery, but who hadn't touched my mother. Right in front of their mother, Fred warned that, if he ever saw either of them within a mile of the store he would break all of their fingers ONE BY ONE. Needless to say, Mother never had any more trouble with them. However, my nephew Jim said that the thief almost strangled a woman who was protecting her son from him after his release from jail, so again he was back in custody. I guess he was really bad news.

Painful as her shoulder was the next day, Mother was even more hurt by the newspaper report. It stated, "an elderly seventy-eight year old woman" was robbed. I think Mother always thought of herself as "forever sixty", so seeing her age in print like that made her sad. She said, "Now all the kids will know how old I am."

Several people asked how I could cope with the coma. They said they could NEVER bear it if it happened to them. I wanted to scream, "How can I not cope with it? I can't make him better and I can't crawl into a hole and die. Please tell me the alternative." But I kept silent because I know I would have made that blind statement to others if the shoe was on the other foot. Until it happens to you, you don't know what you are capable of doing.

CHAPTER 16

Sad to say, one of the biggest disappointments was the attitude of the regular priests of our parish. Although all six of us attended Mass together every Sunday as a family, not one priest entered our home during those difficult twenty-five months to talk things over and see how we were doing. When we met them at Mass they rarely asked for Bobby, just commenting on mundane things like the weather.

I had grown up in close proximity to our church and saw how kind the priests were to those in need. Somehow I thought the same courtesy would be extended to us if ever we needed it, but that was not to be.

Even the hospital chaplain left a lot to be desired. For some strange reason he seemed to think the coma was contagious. He'd dash by our room with barely a nod in our direction. On the occasions when Bobby had an infection and we were required to wear masks upon entering the room, the chaplain would run by the door with a frightened look, almost as if he was being chased by the very devil himself. Bob and I would just look at each other and seethe.

In direct contrast to those priests, on the other hand, was a wonderful young deacon who was temporarily assigned to our church prior to his ordination to the priesthood the following May. Week after week that young deacon would visit us at the hospital for over an hour, lending comfort in his words and prayers. Unlike the chaplain, when we were required to wear masks he wouldn't hesitate a minute. He'd don the mask, come in and bless Bobby, and stay there comforting us. Not much older than Bobby himself, he showed a compassion rare in one so young. The other priests would have done well to emulate him.

One day he came in just after the doctor had given me more bad news. I said, "Who does that doctor think he is? He isn't God. Bobby could wake up tomorrow and that doctor could drop dead, and there would be nothing he could do about it." The poor priest just agreed with me, even though he undoubtedly knew the prognosis wasn't very hopeful.

After Bobby's death some people marveled that we kept up our faith after the way the priests treated Bobby's illness. However, we knew no one was going to take it away from us. Our faith is what helped us to survive and to stay together. We are still here and the others are gone - and the replacement priests are wonderfully helpful and compassionate.

Another person who gave us comfort was a little elderly lady who worked as a domestic in the Intensive Care unit at Salem Hospital. One afternoon I was talking to Bobby as usual when Loretta came in with a kindly smile and went in to clean Bobby's lavatory. When she heard me she looked around the doorway and said, "I'm glad you talk to him because he can hear you, you know." Pleased I said, "Oh, I hope so." She smiled and said, "He does. When I'm here alone I always go over and talk to him and the minute I call his name he turns his head toward me." My heart went out to that compassionate woman. Here she was working at a less than glamorous job, and yet she took the time to be kind to my son, even though he had no real way of responding to her. That happened shortly before Bobby left Salem, and I never had the chance to tell her what her kindness meant to me.

There were some funny moments, too, that helped to relieve the tension. A young intern working in Intensive Care was quite friendly and nice, but he didn't look anything like a doctor. He wore outrageous bow ties that seemed to be his signature, and proudly announced they were made by his wife. We could well believe they were - big and floppy, and made out of a terrible assortment of material, evidently left over from the dresses she made for herself. Someone told me they lived in a trailer on the outer limits of the hospital grounds. He rode his bike in to work, wearing an old ski jacket with a knitted cap drawn down almost to his eyes.

One night the receptionist laughed and said, "Watch this." As the doctor passed through with his head bent low and wearing his ski cap, she said in a loud voice, "Good night, doctor." Every eye in the waiting room looked up in disbelief, wondering how he could be a doctor. The receptionist and I just stood there laughing.

Bobby had a very high temperature one night and that same doctor came into the room. When he explained what the temperature was I asked if he could do anything for him. He said, "Yes, we put him on a cold bedroll and gave him medication - but you don't seem to realize it, Mrs. Hall. He COULD die." Looking him right in the eye I said, "But he ISN'T GOING TO." Then I asked him not to tell me anything at all if it wasn't good news, to just let me live each day as it came. And he did.

CHAPTER 17

We really lost Bobby three times, each one so difficult to take. There were, of course, the days of his accident and of his death. But to my mind the second time we lost him was the worst day of my life. It was when they told us they were moving him to a hospital in Stoughton, fifty miles away.

We knew there was nothing we could do about the accident or his death. Those days were in God's hands. But we so desperately wanted to do something about his move, and yet our hands were tied. They wanted him out of that hospital - PERIOD.

Intensive Care was set up for short-term patients, and Bobby already had the dubious distinction of having spent more time in that unit than any other patient. I suppose subconsciously I knew that once he left Salem he would never again return. And he didn't.

During the month of March, five months into the coma, they paraded an assortment of nurses and therapists in and out of Bobby's room. Their explanation to us was that they were studying his case prior to his move to Shaughnessey

Rehabilitation Hospital, a new facility adjoining Salem Hospital that was built to take care of long-term patients.

Although we didn't feel he was well enough to move anywhere, that was a move we felt we could live with. The same distance from home, only the hospital visiting hours were different. We knew all too well that our days would be worked around his new visiting hours.

On the last Monday in March I was at my usual vigil when the nurses started talking about Bobby's impending move. When I mentioned Shaughnessey, they looked startled and hurried out of the room, but I didn't think anything about it at the time.

That night Bob came home from work and said they had called from the hospital to set up an appointment with the two of us and the doctor the following afternoon. My initial response was that I wasn't going to go. I didn't want to hear ONE MORE PERSON TELL ME OUR SON WAS GOING TO DIE. But I knew I had to attend the meeting. Bob needed my support as much as I needed his, and it wasn't fair to have him go it alone. He told me if they said anything I didn't like I should just get up and walk out of the room.

Tuesday afternoon I went to the hospital right from work, and Bob took the afternoon off to meet me there. Before we were even into the conference room, the social director told Bob they were moving Bobby to the hospital in Stoughton. Shaughnessey wouldn't take him until he was breathing on his own, and they were unable to get him off the respirator. Bob tried to argue with him, but it was in vain.

We entered the conference room and the sour-faced doctor came in. Looking down his nose at us as if we were two senile idiots who had the audacity to question his professional expertise, he said in a cold voice, "You might as well face it, Mr. and Mrs. Hall, the chances of your son coming out of this are zero." ZERO! He couldn't have hurt more had he stabbed me with a knife. But I didn't walk out of the room. Instead, I clenched my fists, bit my lip, and silently vowed that one day our son was going to walk out of that hospital, all six feet two of him, and that damned doctor was going to have to eat his words. I was so sure, but then I had to be. It was the only way I could survive the everyday horror with which I was being forced to live.

We were not senile idiots, we were just desperate parents. When you're desperate you're willing to grasp at any straw, no matter how fragile, hoping against hope that you'll be the one person in a million to realize a miracle. Hope dies hard when the child on that bed is your own.

After the doctor left, the social director added insult to injury when he said, "Mrs. Hall, you have to think of your other children." I could have strangled him. During those five months of hell, about the only thing Bob and I were able to take pride in was the way we had kept things so damned normal for the other children - more normal, if the truth be known, than many homes where they weren't facing a crisis. And yet here was that bozo, who had no idea of our family lifestyle, deeming himself judge and juror of what was best for our children.

Without help from anyone we had kept up on our jobs, the meals, housework and laundry. The children still had their friends in to play games, and we continued to have their special parties, complete with decorated house and cakes. We never missed a family function, again with the handmade and decorated cakes. We were sometimes early or late, working around Bobby's visiting hours, but we never missed a thing. With the family coming down so often, the children had the company of their cousins while the adults went to the hospital. If Jane had a special function with school or Campfire girls, I went with her while Bob and the boys visited the hospital. Conversely, if Larry or Brian had something special to do, Bob went with them and Jane and I visited Bobby. How that social director felt it would be better for them after Bobby's move is beyond my comprehension. It only stood to reason that if we visited him twice daily when he was at Salem, we had no intention of deserting him once he was moved to Stoughton.

It was after that move that our lives were even more disrupted. Larry had a small job working at the bowling alley, so when we spent the long days with Bobby he was often alone. No longer did we have the normal mealtime. Most of our meals were at the Stoughton Diner after our hospital visits. The children couldn't have their cousins down because we were heading in the opposite direction and the longer drive made it almost impossible for the others to visit daily.

I worried about Larry almost as much as I did about Bobby. He seemed so lost and I knew it bothered him to see his brother on that bed. Then, too, I wasn't around as much as I had been, and we didn't have our after-dinner discussions that we used to have. The poor kid seemed to withdraw into himself. How I hated the machine at that garage for causing our family so much grief.

When the social director came up with that stupid remark, I just left the room in disgust. Entering Bobby's room I found Jayne, one of our favorite nurses, working on him. Alternating between crying and seething I moaned, "I wonder what that damned doctor would do if it was his wife on that bed and I was the cold-hearted doctor." Her answer shook me to the core: "He'd pull the plug." After that, all I wanted was to get Bobby out of there. Heartbroken I asked her what she would do if she was in my shoes. She was honest in her answer. She said, "Speaking as a nurse I'd say it was hopeless. Speaking as a mother I would never give up." And I knew she understood.

Bob came into the room a few minutes later and after our visit with Bobby we went home to the difficult task of telling the other children. We knew it wouldn't be easy. They had suffered so much over those months, and the minute they saw our faces they didn't say a word. They knew it was bad.

We went into the living room where Bob explained what was happening. Jane screamed, "They can't take my brother away from me. It just isn't fair." I thought, "FAIR! Oh, honey, nothing has been fair during this whole horrible nightmare." Larry just sat there, silent in his grief, but I knew he was hurting so much. Jane's outburst was Bob's undoing. He just sat in his chair and bawled. It was the blackest moment of my life. All those months he had kept his heartache to himself, trying to be strong for the rest of us. But even the strongest have their breaking point, and this was Bob's. He was the kind of father who gave fatherhood his all - getting involved in every aspect of the children's lives, being there when they needed him. They knew if anything troubled them they needed only to talk to him and he would make it right. Now he couldn't help Bobby and he felt so defeated.

Within minutes, however, he was back in command of the situation. He sat Jane on his knee and quietly explained that perhaps we owed it to Bobby to have him moved. Salem had him for five months with no noticeable change, and the move to Stoughton might be just what was needed to get him back on the road to recovery. Jane listened intently and then the rapid-fire questions began.

"Will we be able to see the hospital before they move Bobby?

"Yes, Jane, Tomorrow you and Larry can stay out of school and we'll all go down to look the place over."

"Will you talk to the doctors and nurses and ask them to be good to Bobby?"

"I'll tell them I want them to do everything in their power to keep him comfortable and get him on the road to recovery."

"Will you talk to the therapists and ask them if they can get Bobby off the respirator so he can come back to Shaughnessey?"

"I'll tell them I never want them to stop trying to get him breathing on his own."

And then the most important question of them all, "Will they let me visit Bobby at this new hospital?"

On that, Bob was adamant. He said, "Jane, I'll never again allow anyone to keep you from seeing Bobby."

Then, with the ability she always had to set things straight in her mind and make a decision, she said, "Then I think it's right that we have him moved."

I marveled at that. Here at my age my mind was going in a million directions at once while she, at the age of nine, already had her mind set on what was best. Her faith and strength were an inspiration to all of us.

We then had the difficult task of telling Brian and the rest of the family. We are such a close family that I knew they ached over every bit of bad news almost as much as we did.

That night when we visited Bobby even the nurses and therapists were crying. I couldn't help feeling we were deserting our son, but it was out of our hands. Most of the family came down and Bobby's girl Pat and her parents also came over. Later we had coffee at our house and tried to cheer each other up, but I suppose we all knew by then that it was the beginning of the end.

Wednesday morning we headed for Stoughton, and even the beautiful summer-like day did little to lift our spirits. As each endless mile passed by we realized just how far they were taking him from us. When we arrived at the hospital we saw it was a new facility, in a nice enough surrounding, but even that did little to bolster our spirits. And what a snow job they gave us at that hospital! As they showed us around they told us they got the patients up into orthopedic chairs and took them around the hospital. They said they had concerts in the lounge and would even take the comatose patients, complete with portable respirators, down to the room to see if the music would have any effect on them. What propaganda that was. In his twenty months at that hospital, he never left the room. In fact, I never even heard of a concert being held there during his stay.

That was the beginning of another routine. Saturdays and Sundays we spent with Bobby, and on Monday, my day off, I took Mother down to visit him. At night we'd drive back home where my brother Fred and his wife Kay came down for coffee and took Mother home. Usually we all went down right after Bob got home from work on Wednesday. Sometimes we would go on other nights, but always managed to be there at least four days a week.

Little did we realize that hospital would be like going from the frying pan into the fire. Everything that could go wrong did, and much of it was caused by human error. I am not so naive as to think that Bobby would have lived if things had been handled differently, but I do know they caused him, and us, endless misery.

As the summer months approached, we had other concerns - what to do with Jane and Larry while we were at the hospital so far away. We didn't think it was fair to have them spending all that time in those surroundings. They were young and needed to live their own lives. My sister Rita and her husband Steve Goveia came up with the solution.

During the winter Steve was athletic director in a high school on Cape Cod and Rita was a school nurse. Summers they closed their home and moved to a farmhouse on a children's camp just south of Boston where Steve was assistant director and Rita was the camp nurse.

One night Rita called and said Steve wanted Larry to be a camp counselor and she asked if Jane could spend the summer with her and her children. She might just as well have given me a million dollars. It was just the answer to our prayers. Both children jumped at the offer and had a wonderful summer.

We'd drive down to see them after visiting Bobby and when we got there, Larry was always surrounded by kids. He had a great time with them and we knew they liked and respected him as their counselor. Jane, of course, loved being with her cousins, and we knew Rita and Steve would keep as close a watch on them as Bob and I did.

During the winter months my sister Gay and her husband Bob McEvoy came to our rescue. They had Jane and Larry up there many weekends so they could enjoy their cousins. It was a great help to us and saved us worrying about them.

The following year Bobby was still in the hospital, so they were invited to the camp again where they enjoyed the summer with their cousins. The camp had two olympic-sized pools and a lake and boats, and they had a lot of fun. Brian was busy working, so that left Bob and me free to go to the hospital as often as possible.

CHAPTER 18

During the first month at Stoughton, Bob and I went in on a warm Sunday afternoon and Bobby was perspiring heavily. We kept asking them to change his linens, but they were short of nurses and kept putting us off. At the time we were new to the hospital and hesitated to change him ourselves because of all the wires attached to him. On later visits we went right ahead and took care of him if things weren't as we wanted them to be. But leaving him that way caused a bedsore on his back that showed up awhile later and caused him all sorts of trouble.

They moved him to a semi-private room where an older man was also in a coma. His name was Joe Molino, and his wife Ann and son Joe, Jr. became two of our closest friends. They had another son, but he was away at college and only came occasionally. Young Joe, however, was faithfully there every night, working his dates around the visiting hours. He and Brian became close friends and remain friends to this day.

Ann and I tended to stay in the room, but Jane and Bob would roam the corridors and meet other people. Jane was terrific. She became friends with all the others and visited them when the nurses were working on Bobby. She became the favorite at the hospital. When Bobby died Ann said everyone at the hospital was more concerned about how Jane took it than about how Bob and I did. She had to grow up quickly, and she was certainly was up to the task.

At the hospital we met a woman named Pauline who would put us all to shame. Her son Billy was also in a coma as a result of an automobile accident. She didn't work, so she was there every day and kept an eye out for all the patients. She had a very upbeat disposition which I have no doubt hid a lot of heartache. She must have done her crying in private.

Because Bobby was on the respirator, they never took him out in the chair. Her Billy, however, wasn't on a respirator, so every warm day she'd have them put him in a chair and she'd take him outside. No bigger than a minute, she'd push that heavy orthopedic chair all around the hospital grounds with Billy wearing a baseball cap. He got a little color from the sun and looked much healthier when he was back in bed. Sadly, like the rest of them, he didn't survive.

Pauline's problems were also compounded by her broken marriage and her lack of money, but you'd never know it the way she kept everyone's spirits up. She was quite a woman.

In the room with Billy was a young fellow named Paul, whose parents never came to see him. We were shocked to see a postcard on his bulletin board from the parents, who were vacationing in the Caribbean. It said, "Having a great time, wish you were here." We couldn't believe it, and it was the talk of the parents in our section. I guess that was their way of coping with his illness.

One day when I arrived at the hospital, Ann said one of the other mothers had mentioned to the nurse how cruel that card was. The nurse took her to task. She said, "They are the realistic ones. They know Paul is going to die and are going on with their lives. You people are the unrealistic ones." After that none of us voiced our opinions. There is really no "right" or "wrong" way in a situation like that. Each family has to face it in the only way comfortable for them.

CHAPTER 19

As 1977 came to an end and we realized we were facing our second Christmas without Bobby, it seemed hard to believe. I think a blessed kind of numbness sets in so that you can function normally every day as if in a semi-dream. Bobby was doing reasonably well on Christmas, but he had another setback on New Year's Eve, which kept us at the hospital quite late. We had planned on taking the children out to dinner after the hospital visit, and it was close to midnight when we finally got our dinner. It was hardly a pleasant beginning for a new year.

It brought to mind another New Year's Eve. Bob and I were at a party in Somerville and Bobby and his girl went to New Hampshire to celebrate with all his cousins. We stayed quite late at the club because they had coffee and donuts long after midnight. When we left the club it was snowing and quite a bit had accumulated. All the way home I worried about Bobby driving in the snow that long distance from New Hampshire. The minute we got into the driveway he came running out saying he had been worried about US.

PATRICIA HALEY HALL

In early January we had a very serious setback. There was such a turnover of doctors at that hospital, most of them foreigners with heavy accents, that it made it difficult to understand them. On Monday Jane and I were planning on taking my mother to the hospital, but in mid-morning we had a call from the doctor. He mumbled something about Bobby's blood pressure going drastically low, and his condition was serious. Frantic, I tried to get him to speak more clearly. Finally I realized he was trying to say Bobby had a blood infection. I called Mother and told her we wouldn't be up, that we had to rush right down to the hospital.

They had called Bob at his office and a few minutes later he came running in. He said the doctor told him, "This is it," and that we'd better hurry right down to the hospital. We decided to stop at the high school and take Larry with us.

Several times during Bobby's illness a woman in Bob's Washington office sent us soothing cards with HELEN STEINER RICE poems on them. One of them became my Bible, and I memorized it. All the way to the hospital I kept repeating it over and over again in silence, hoping some kind of miracle would meet us at the hospital. The poem was as follows:

"THIS TOO WILL PASS AWAY"

If I can endure for this minute
Whatever is happening to me
No matter how heavy my heart is
Or how "dark" the moment may be

If I can remain calm and quiet
With all my world crashing about me,
Secure in the knowledge God loves me,
When everyone else seems to doubt me.
If I can but keep on believing
What I know in my heart to be true,
That "darkness will fade with the morning"
And that THIS WILL PASS AWAY, TOO,
Then nothing in life can defeat me
For as long as this knowledge remains
I can suffer whatever is happening
For I know God will break "all the chains"
That are binding me tight in "THE DARKNESS"
And trying to fill me with fear
For there is NO NIGHT WITHOUT DAWNING
And I know that "MY MORNING" is near.
HELEN STEINER RICE

The previous Saturday evening, just before we left the hospital, we noticed there were bubbles coming out of Bobby's tracheotomy tube and we knew there was a leak in the cuff around his neck. Bob mentioned it to the therapists, who arrived just as we were leaving. Naturally we thought they would be changing him to a new respirator.

He hadn't looked good on Sunday, but we were unprepared for such a drastic change. Arriving at the hospital we were met by the head doctor who was offering all kinds of apologies, which surprised us. We knew it was something they were responsible for. Later we found out that they hadn't changed the respirator that Saturday night, Bobby aspirated into the tube, causing it to go down into his lungs. That is what caused his pressure to drop drastically. Amazingly he pulled through that crisis and was with us for almost another year.

A few weeks after that incident one of the respiratory therpists, who had been on duty that Saturday night, came in to look at Bobby's machine. I mentioned something about not wanting it to ever happen again. She seemed amazed when I told her the doctor had admitted they were wrong. I never saw her again after that and heard she had transferred to another hospital.

In July of 1978 we had another new head doctor assigned to the hospital and the social director set up a meeting with Bob, me, and the new doctor. Bob went, but I refused to go. Later on the doctor showed up at our room saying he wanted to meet me. After he left the room, the social director said she was worried about me and that I should take a vacation. I couldn't believe it! We had made it clear from the start that we weren't giving up on Bobby, so I don't know how she thought we would enjoy a vacation. She seemed aggravated that I wouldn't talk my troubles over with her, but I had my family to confide in and they brought me comfort.

CHAPTER 20

Even the elements were against us. We had an ice storm in January 1977 that took us two hours to make the ten-minute drive to Salem Hospital. The cities had sanded the streets earlier in the day, but the icy rain washed it away and driving on the streets became treacherous. When the main roads were closed off, Bob tried all the side streets, and even the slightest incline had us slipping back down the hill. It was a miserable ride, and once we got to the hospital we decided to stay until visiting hours were over at night. We called the children and told them to have a sandwich and we'd get supper when we got home.

Then in May of that same year Mother and I were caught in a surprise snowstorm while visiting Bobby in Stoughton. All the snow-fighting equipment had been put away for the summer, so we drove fifty miles on a snow-filled highway, sliding and skidding along the way. It was a nightmare and I was glad to arrive in Peabody. Only when we exited in Peabody did I see a sand truck entering the highway.

We had two of what were, to us, the hottest summers on record. At the time we didn't have air conditioning in the cars, and driving on that hot asphalt with the sun beating down made it quite uncomfortable. We bought an air-conditioned car in August of 1978, but within a few months Bobby was gone.

But the most devastating of all had to be the crippling blizzard of 1978. For the first time in the history of Massachusetts, the governor was forced to close the entire eastern part of the state. All schools, offices, businesses and stores were closed, and only official vehicles were allowed on the highways. A few supermarkets remained open for emergencies. Bob found an old sled in the shed and we pulled it up to the supermarket for supplies.

The worst part of all was that we were kept from seeing Bobby for a week. Thank God he didn't have a crisis during that time, or I think I would have gone crazy. Even our phone calls had to be curtailed, because the hospital was operating with an emergency crew and the hospital recreation and reception rooms were being used to accommodate the stranded motorists. Some nurses and doctors stayed all week. Snowmobiles and National Guard trucks brought in additional replacements

That snowstorm could have been a disaster for our family. On Sunday evening we drove Bob to the airport on the way home from the hospital because he had to be in New York early Monday morning to attend the fish auction at Fulton Fish Market. Monday morning I heard on the news that they had a snowstorm in New York and LaGuardia Airport was closed down. I thought that meant Bob would be spending another night in New York. When he didn't call I figured the lines were tied up with the storm.

I called Mother to tell her I would be up to take her to the hospital. She sounded apprehensive about the impending storm, but it wasn't snowing at the time and I thought we would have plenty of time to visit before the storm hit Massachusetts. I knew if the car was going she would be determined to go.

As I turned from one highway onto another leading to Lowell, I heard on the car radio that a truck had jackknifed at the Stoughton exit and traffic there was backing up onto the highway. I knew it would take me over an hour to pick Mother up and get down to that exit, so I thought the truck would be removed by that time. Suddenly snow flurries started, but they just blew across the road. Nothing had accumulated. For some strange reason, however, my car did a spin and turned completely around. Fortunately I have never been a nervous driver and was able to control the car. But that spin made up my mind for me. I turned at the next exit and headed back to Peabody. I know Mother breathed a sigh of relief when I called to tell her we wouldn't be going.

Jane had a dress rehearsal at the high school that afternoon. The high school drama club was putting on a presentation of "THE KING AND I" and they were using the grammar school children as the children of the king. Jane was one of those chosen. When I thought I'd be heading to Stoughton, another mother offered to drive the girls home. I called to tell her I'd pick them up instead, because I wasn't going to Stoughton. By the time I arrived at the school the snow was really piling up. I was grateful when we got to our driveway and we were home for the evening.

Bob still hadn't called, but I thought the lines were tied up in New York and that he'd call later that night. About eight o'clock I heard a car door slam and was astonished when he walked into the house. He said the auction was over when he heard on the radio that the airport was closed, so he took a cab to the train station and got on the last train out of New York. It took him all day to get here, but he made it. If he hadn't come home then, we wouldn't have seen him for a week.

The next day the newspapers showed hundreds of cars stranded on the highway, many of them at the Stoughton exit where the truck had jackknifed. If my car hadn't skidded, Mother and I would undoubtedly have been in one of those stranded cars. God was with us, and I believe He is the one who caused the skid and made me return to Peabody.

Jane's show was held the following week and many of the family came down to attend. We visited Bobby that afternoon, but didn't get there at night because of the play. Jane didn't have any lines to speak, but she was proud to have been chosen for the small part she did have. Like most school plays, it gave us a lot of laughs, which was just what we needed at that particular time.

CHAPTER 21

In July of 1978 we had even more trouble, this one having nothing to do with Bobby, either. As a counselor at camp, Larry had one day off in ten - leaving camp at 7:00 one morning and returning at 7:00 the next. He was scheduled to be home on a Friday and I was surprised he wasn't there when I returned home from work in the afternoon. Just before suppertime he came in, covered with grease from head to toe.

His muffler had fallen from his car, and he had spent most of the day trying to tie it up all the way home, stopping often along the way as it slipped off again and again. We knew he needed a newer car, but none of us had the time to go out and look for one. I told him to take a shower and when Bob came home at night he would decide what to do.

After supper Bob said the only thing we could do was have a new muffler put on for the time being. He and Larry went out, but no garage would do it on a Friday night. They told him to come back on Saturday morning.

I offered to drive him back to camp early Saturday morning. Brian, wanting to save me the trip when he knew we had the long drive to the hospital that afternoon, volunteered to have Larry take his car back to camp. He and his girlfriend had Monday off, so he said they would drive Larry's car down on Monday, after it was fixed, and they could exchange cars.

Sunday morning we were just leaving for church when the phone rang and it was Larry. He sounded dazed as he told us he had totaled the car the previous night. With that my sister Rita grabbed the phone and said, "Pat, don't say a word. You'll never know how close we came to having a double fatality in the family last night." Rita's daughter Lisa was with Larry at the time of the accident. Rita said Larry had a concussion, and the only reason he wasn't in the hospital was because she was a nurse and had promised to keep a close eye on him. She said he was hurting and only wanted to rest, but she made him call because she knew we would panic if we didn't hear his voice.

After the campers were in bed that Saturday night, and only the roving counselors were on duty, the other counselors gathered in the lounge. It was a hot night and they were restless, and someone mentioned they'd like a pizza. Larry had the only car available, so they piled into the car and headed for the pizza parlor.

The camp is located deep among the woods with no street lights in sight. They had driven past the pizza parlor before realizing it, because it was set back among the trees. Larry backed into a driveway to turn around. He didn't see anyone coming, so he pulled out into the road. Meanwhile, a van had pulled out of the pizza parking lot with the lights out. Just as the driver put them on, he saw Larry in front of him. He hit them broadside, pushing them thirty yards down the road.

Larry passed out and when Lisa saw him she thought he was dead. She went running down that dark road screaming. Fortunately one of the camp officials was driving down the road at the time. He picked her up and went back to the scene of the accident. In addition to the concussion, Larry had bruises all over his left side. Only the fact that they were packed into the car so closely saved them from worse injuries. They acted as buffers for each other, and no one was thrown from the car. Larry, with a concussion, was hurt the most seriously. The others were just shaken up. Rita said they were up all night, and she said she was keeping him in her apartment for awhile so she could keep her eye on him.

When we got out of Mass we headed straight for the camp. I stayed with Rita while Bob and Brian went down to see the car and to get the report from the police station. From what I understand, the other driver was cited for having liquor in the van. But when I saw the pictures of the damaged car I was sick. We so easily could have lost another son. I remember asking God, "Do we have to make up for our thirty years of good luck in one fell swoop?" It seemed like everything in our lives was going wrong.

I was torn between wanting to stay with Larry that afternoon, and going to the hospital to visit Bobby. But we stayed for the afternoon trying to comfort him, even though he probably only wanted to sleep. By the time we arrived at the hospital, visiting hours were almost over and Ann Molino

PATRICIA HALEY HALL
was in a panic. When we didn't show up at the hospital she called the house. With no one answering the phone, she thought we had been in an accident on the way down to the hospital. All the other people were concerned, and they felt terrible when they heard about Larry. I guess by then all we could do was roll with the punches.

CHAPTER 22

One day in September of 1978 we visited Bobby and saw he was again on the cold bedroll. The bedsore on his back had flared up and he was on new medication to help bring the temperature down. We were worried and visited him every day for almost a week. One night I stayed home with Jane while Bob went down alone.

Ann Molino called me about 9:30 and was practically in tears. She said she felt so sad for Bob that night. When he arrived at the hospital he noticed they had pulled the private nurses from Bobby's case. He questioned Dolores, the head nurse on that wing. She said if we wanted private nurses to cover him we had to hire them ourselves.

We didn't come from that area, knew no one around there except the hospital personnel, and Bob had no idea of where he would hire a nurse at that hour. She, on the other hand, had all that information right at her fingertips. Bob was afraid to come home and leave Bobby alone. Finally, in desperation, he went to Dolores and told her if anything happened to Bobby that night he was going to hold her personally responsible. That shook her and she promised he would be covered. Bob arrived home about midnight and was visibly shaken.

The whole month of September was a nightmare for us. Bobby had an infection and was running a high temp so they put him on medication. One Sunday afternoon we went in and he seemed warm, but no one said anything to us about it. One of the women visiting her son-in-law in the adjoining room said something had happened during the afternoon and they were running in and out of the room, even changing Bobby's respirator. That seemed a bit unusual for a Sunday afternoon. We tried to get information out of the nurses at the desk, but they said we would have to wait another day until the doctor came in.

When Mother and I went in on Monday, Bobby still seemed warm and we were quite concerned, but again they wouldn't tell us what was happening - only that he had the infection and was on medication.

Wednesday night we went to the hospital and two different people said they were sorry Bobby had pneumonia. That shocked us, so Bob checked at the desk. They said he didn't have pneumonia. Exasperated, Bob said he was going to get to the bottom of what was going on.

The next morning he was concerned and called the hospital before heading to his office in Gloucester. First they told him they could no longer give information out on the phone about Bobby's condition. Then Bob asked them to contact the doctor. This time the call was disconnected and he was furious. Bob rang right back, insisted they NOT hang up on him, and said he would be in his office within the hour. He said he expected the doctor to call him by then or he would be right down to the hospital demanding to see the director.

Shortly after Bob arrived at his office, the doctor called. It was a new one we had never met. She told Bob that Bobby DIDN'T have pneumonia. When Bob asked what had happened to the respirator the previous Sunday she bristled and asked who had told him about it - one of the nurses? It wasn't, but Bob didn't tell her who had told him. He asked to speak to the head doctor. She was livid and told him SHE was the doctor and would answer all his questions. He then told her he would call anyone necessary if he couldn't get the right answers from her. She promised to call him right back, but she didn't, so Bob called the social services director to complain. Finally the doctor reluctantly returned his call and said Bobby DIDN'T have pneumonia but was on intravenous injections. When Bob questioned when he was put on IVs, she said it was on Wednesday afternoon. Bob informed her we were down on Wednesday evening and he WAS NOT on IVs. She then made a call on her other line and got back to Bob saying he was not on IVs, but DID have pneumonia - a complete reversal of what she had just reported. Some doctor!!

Bob was furious and insisted on speaking to the head doctor, saying that if he didn't get results he would be right down to settle it. That got action and the head doctor got on the phone. What he said shocked us. He said Bobby didn't have pneumonia, but had a reaction from too much medication. The previous doctor had left him on it for five extra days, causing him all kinds of problems. The overdose had caused him to turn blue the previous Sunday afternoon. I was amazed a doctor would even admit it, and we were so upset.

We also learned later that one of the night nurses, who had worked diligently to clear up Bobby's bedsore on his back, had been fired. I believe it was because they thought she had told us about the respirator. In retrospect, I wish I had found out her name, but shortly after that incident Bobby died and all I wanted to do was forget about that hospital.

Upset as were about everything that was happening there, there was really nothing we could do about it. One time Bob complained they told him we could always move him if we were dissatisfied. But we knew we couldn't. The only other hospital accepting respiratory patients at the time was in Springfield, a much further distance from our home than Stoughton. Our hands were tied.

CHAPTER 23

Again, in September of 1978 we visited Bobby on a Sunday afternoon. Bob left me off at the door and went to park the car. It was a dark afternoon and as soon as I turned the corner of his corridor I heard a bell ringing and I was sure it was on Bobby's respirator. I flew down that corridor and was shocked when I got to the room. It had always been highly lit. That afternoon, however, the room was in darkness, the respirator was buzzing off the wall, and Bobby was gagging with the congestion coming up into his tube.

I lit the lights and then ran down the corridor yelling for a nurse to suction him, but there was NO ONE in sight. The desk was empty, the supervisor was gone, and all those critically ill patients were without coverage. Finally I saw a woman in white and asked her to take care of Bobby. She was only an LPN and said she wasn't supposed to suction him. By then Bob had arrived and he demanded she do it, and she did. Then he went back down the corridor looking for someone who was in charge. One by one the nurses and therapists wandered in from their meal. I couldn't believe they would all disappear and leave those critically ill patients unattended.

Earlier Bob had suggested the respiratory patients all be placed on one wing where the therapists could keep an eye on them, but they ignored the suggestion. Like everything else that happened at that hospital, it was a nightmare.

I found that we weren't the only ones with complaints so I wrote a long letter to the social director listing all the complaints from us and the others. They notified us they were holding a meeting with the personnel and families of the patients on a Friday night. Brian decided to come with us. He had visited Bobby the previous Friday afternoon when he left school, and was disgusted with the way Bobby looked. The bed hadn't been cleaned and the hospital gown he was wearing didn't look fresh. He was livid. Bobby had always been fastidious and it was heartbreaking to see him otherwise.

When we got to the conference room we were surprised to see a nurse we had never seen, and she announced that she was the hospital's director of nurses. Even the courageous mother Pauline, who spent day and night there, was surprised because she had never seen that nurse in the hospital. After giving a short speech to introduce herself, she went around the room asking the people about their concerns. I was amazed at their complaints - faded johnnies, cold meals being served, and other little things. Our complaints were: not answering the alarm bells, over medication, and more serious charges.

They got to Brian before Bob, and I was going to suggest he let Bob do the talking, but he was furious and wanted to tell them what he thought about the condition he found Bobby in. And he did. When Bob got up he asked why they had the agency nurses on Bobby instead of the regular nurses, when they knew how critical he was. Her answer infuriated us. She said, "We have to pay so much for the agency nurses we want to get our money's worth out of them." I felt like exploding. Bobby's expenses were being paid by the insurance company, while many of the others were on welfare, and yet he was getting less service than the others. With that, I just left the room in disgust and went back to Bobby's room.

A few minutes later I was stunned when a woman I had never seen before barged into the room and said, "I don't know what you wrote, but I want to thank you because I've been here for three years and never saw that head nurse and I have a lot of complaints about how they are taking care of my mother. Thank you." With that she barged right out of the room, almost knocking Bob over as he returned from the meeting. I asked him what that was all about. He said she had come late to the meeting, refused to sit down when they offered her a seat, and when they came to her she yelled about all the things that were wrong and then just stormed right out of the room. I guess we weren't the only ones who were dissatisfied.

CHAPTER 24

On the Tuesday before Thanksgiving of 1978 we stayed a little late at the hospital because Bobby had just gotten over another infection. We knew we wouldn't be down on Wednesday night because we planned on spending all Thanksgiving day at the hospital. Ann Molino stayed late with us. She and I were talking by Joe's bed as Bob washed Bobby's teeth and combed his hair. Suddenly Bob called and we went running over to the bed. With what must have been a superhuman effort for someone in a coma, Bobby had sat bolt upright in bed. Bob immediately braced his back with his arm. Eye to eye with his father, and with his eyes as big as saucers, Bobby seemed to be trying to talk, and his mouth moved back and forth.

Although I knew Bob was excited beyond measure, his voice was calm as he said, "Bobby, you can't talk now because you have a tube in your throat, but I'll ask the doctor to take it out and then you can talk to me." Still Bobby kept staring at him trying to mouth some words. Then he slumped back against the pillows - as deep in the coma as ever.

But that didn't discourage us. It was the best sign we had seen in twenty-five months and we were elated. He was trying to talk; he was coming out of the coma!!

The three of us went out of the hospital that night in high spirits. After all, we were beginning to see the start of our miracle. All the way home Bob was beside himself with excitement. He said, "On Thanksgiving day I'm going to ask the doctor to remove the tube so that Bobby can talk." We were so sure. I went around doing the Thanksgiving shopping on Wednesday with a light step, the happiest I had been in months. But my happiness was short-lived.

Thanksgiving morning the boys skipped the ballgame because it was a dull and dreary day. At noon my brother Fred brought Mother down for dinner, and then went back home for the family dinner. He said he'd drive down to the hospital at night for a visit, then we could go out for coffee and he would drive Mother home.

A few minutes after he left, the phone rang and Jane answered it. She called to Bob, who was downstairs in the family room, and said, "It's for you and it sounds serious." i grabbed the kitchen phone and couldn't believe what I was hearing. It was the doctor. He said Bobby had had a setback, and then he described everything they had tried. After each one of them he said, "But it didn't work. I'm sorry." Finally it dawned on me what he was saying. I screamed, "You mean he's gone?" And then the terrible confirmation - "Yes."

I dropped the phone and sank to the chair. I could hear the children screaming in the background. My mother, forgetting her own heartache, ran out to the kitchen to try to comfort me. Then my mind started playing tricks on me. I thought, "I must have heard wrong. Bob will walk up those stairs in a minute and tell me that I misunderstood." One look at his face, however, and there was no doubt. He looked as if part of him had died, and I believe it did. You can't live through a nightmare like that without it taking a toll on you.

Bob went upstairs to make some calls and the rest of us just sat in the living room, numb with shock. Then he came down and said he was going to the church, undertaker, and down to the hospital. Brian insisted on going with him, and he stuck with Bob the whole time. He was such a comfort.

As we sat there so disconsolate, I looked at Larry and he looked devastated. I couldn't believe our safe little world had collapsed so completely. Midway through the afternoon I thought of Ann Molino. I knew what a shock it would be if she went to the hospital and Bobby was gone. I tried to get her on the phone, but there was no answer. A little later the doorbell rang and she and her two sons came in. I should have realized Bob would have called her. Much as they wanted to be with their Joe that day, she said she just couldn't face the hospital after hearing about Bobby. Poor Joe died a month later.

I didn't know what we were going to do, and then Mother asked if we wanted to put Bobby in with my father, the grandfather he had never known. It was such a relief for us and we were so grateful. I couldn't face going to the cemetery to pick out a funeral plot on that cold winter day. It would have been the last straw. That night the whole family came down, trying to give us comfort; but nothing could comfort us then. It was all over.

The day of the funeral dawned dull and overcast - in tune with our feelings. Even with the threat of a major snowstorm, our families all made it, some from clear across the state. They were with us from the beginning, and never failed us at the end.

We had one bad moment upon entering the church when I thought Jane was going to faint. I think it was the sight of her entire class across the aisle from us. But she rallied and was all right for the rest of the day.

There are two major roads heading to Lowell. I always took the main one, and just assumed that would be the route the undertaker would be using. As we crossed over the highway and continued down the road, I stiffened. Bob just squeezed my hand and said everything would be okay, that I should just look to the left. That route was taking us right past the garage where Bobby was killed - a road I had studiously avoided taking since the day of the accident.

But I didn't look away. I looked to the right and what I saw sickened me. With every light ablaze in that place, they were open for business as usual. Open for business!! They didn't even have the decency to close for the hour of his funeral, even though he had been killed at that garage and they were charged with defective machinery. To add insult to injury, NOT ONE PERSON from the garage attended his wake or funeral. Something like that is very hard to forgive. Many of the people working there that day had been with Bobby at the time of the accident. I should think their conscience would bother them.

Our first home was right near the cemetery, but it had slipped my mind. When we got there and I saw those streets

100

where I had walked Bobby in his carriage with such dreams of the beautiful life he would have, I couldn't believe it was all over so soon. How could anything that bad have happened to our once happy family? What had we ever done that was so terrible to have made us deserve this?

When we returned to the house my brother Fred was trying to keep things lightened up and he said something funny. I remember laughing at what he said and I couldn't believe it. One "me" seemed to be looking on from the sidelines. It was a weird feeling I had often during those difficult months.

The families left a littler earlier than they had planned because the snow was starting to accumulate quickly and they had a long ride ahead of them. Bob and the children went up to bed, but I have never been able to sleep in the daytime so I sat alone in the living room. And then it hit me.

As I sat there trying to make some kind of sense out of what had happened to us, it dawned on me what Bobby was trying to tell us on that Tuesday evening. He was telling us that he was giving up, that it was too much for him. He was trying to say "Goodbye."

PATRICIA HALEY HALL

CHAPTER 25

We wanted to do something in Bobby's name and Brian said he heard Peabody was purchasing a new Jaws of Life. When Bob spoke to the fire chief he was told Peabody already had the funds that were donated by others, but that they needed the cutting tools, so Bob gave them the money to purchase them in Bobby's name. But we wanted something more than that. My nephew Jim Quealy, a Lowell fireman, said Lowell needed a new Jaws, so we decided to donate one in Bobby's and my father's name. The following article was printed in THE LOWELL SUN on March 13, 1979.

A living memorial

Robert Hall, left, and James Quealy, nephew of Mrs. Hall, discuss the Halls $7,000 contribution to the Lowell Fire Department to purchase a "jaws of life" rescue tool. The donation is in memory of their son, who was killed in an industrial accident, and his grandfather, the late Capt. James Haley of the Lowell Fire Department.

In memory of son
Peabody couple donates funds for "jaws of life" tool for Lowell

By PATRICIA MONTMINY
Sun Staff

LOWELL — Several months ago, Robert and Patricia Hall of Peabody lost their son in an industrial accident — an accident similar to ones which others have survived with the help of rescue tools like the "jaws of life".

As a memorial to their 23-year-old son, and his grandfather, the late Lowell Fire Department Capt. James Haley, the Halls are donating $7,000 to the Lowell Fire Department to purchase a Lucas Rescue Tool, an improved version of the "jaws of life".

"We felt this donation would be a way of remembering our son, and saving lives," Hall said.

The Halls' son died of injuries sustained in an accident in 1976 at a North Shore auto dealership. The young man was operating a payloader when the bucket came down, crushing his chest. He was on a respirator for 23 months, but never regained consciousness.

During the long agonizing months that followed the accident the Halls came to know many other people whose loved ones were hurt in accidents and comatose. The importance of time and proper equipment in saving lives inspired the Halls into considering something they could do for their son and other people.

THEIR INTEREST in purchasing a piece of equipment for a fire department stemmed from the fact that Mrs. Hall's father, Capt. Haley, devoted his life to helping people, and following in his footsteps is his grandson Lowell Firefighter James Quealy, nephew of Mrs. Hall.

ROBERT J. HALL

The Halls initially looked toward making a contribution to their own community fire department, but Peabody was already in the process of raising funds for a second jaws of life. They completed the fundraising with a $1,000 donation.

However, they wanted to make a donation that would be strictly in memory of their son and Capt. Haley. After discussing their ideas with Quealy, a member of the fire department's rescue squad, who told them that Lowell only had one jaws of life, they decided to ask Lowell Fire Chief John Mulligan if they could make a donation to Lowell, Mrs. Hall's hometown.

"WE DON'T GET a gift like this too often," said Chief Mulligan. "Excluding the mobile units, it is the single most expensive item."

Mulligan looked at a number of devices, but chose the Lucas tool. "It's a lighter version of the jaws, and has

JAMES HALEY

manual back up power." The tool can cut through a steering post in less than a minute, Mulligan noted.

The Lucas tool, which is currently being used on a consignment basis, was delivered to the Lowell Fire Department for a demonstration several weeks ago.

Late this past week the Halls gave the check to Quealy to turn over to the city solicitor to be turned over to the city council.

The Halls have two other sons, Brian, 20, and Lawrence, 18, and a daughter, Jane, 12. Mrs. Hall's mother, who was the wife of the late Capt. Haley, resides in Lowell on 15 Courtland St., where she runs a small variety store.

According to Fire Chief Mulligan, the Hall donation is the largest donation to the fire department in 30 years. He noted that the last donation was a portable iron lung, donated by a community service agency three decades ago. The iron lung is still part of fire department equipment.

Another generous donation, about 30 years ago, Mulligan pointed out, was an ambulance given to the fire department by the American Legion. Mulligan said that it was donated during the period of time that the Lowell Fire Department ran the ambulance service.

"Occasionally we do receive checks for services rendered at fires from kindhearted people," Mulligan said. "Usually the checks range from $25 to $200 and they are normally assigned to the the Lowell Firefighter's Relief Association."

PATRICIA HALEY HALL

CHAPTER 26

We know there are people who are critical of the decision we made to keep Bobby on a respirator all those months, who thought it would have been more merciful to let him die in peace. Some have even come forward and told us, if it was their son, they would have had the plug pulled as soon as the doctor told them it was hopeless.

I pointed out to them that it WASN'T their son, they WEREN'T faced with that decision, and until they were there was no way on earth they could tell what they would or would not do. No one knows better than I the truth of that statement.

During that fateful fall of 1976 I had enrolled in a legal course at our local college. The main assignment for the semester was to select a legal case that had been written up in the newspapers. We were to follow it from the beginning to the end. Then we were to present it in class giving the pros, cons, decision of the court and our own opinion. Later there would be a class discussion and each student would have to give his or her own opinion.

Although the assignment wasn't due until mid-December, one student was anxious to get it out of the way and decided to present her report to the class on Thursday evening, October 21st. The case she reported on was 'THE KAREN QUINLAN CASE" where the parents went to court in an effort to have their comatose daughter removed from the life supporting respirator. How well I remember my opinion on that long ago pre-accident Thursday: "No wonder they want to have the respirator removed. After all, the doctors TOLD them it was hopeless." I had no way of knowing that, just two days hence, we would be faced with that momentous decision, and there was no way on earth we could consent to having the plug removed. It's one thing when you're talking about some stranger in a remote hospital bed miles away, but quite another story when the child on that bed is your own. We know we made the only decision we could comfortably live with for the rest of our lives, and with that we will have to be content.

Nothing in life prepares you for the death of a child - a handsome, healthy, vital child. You go through life believing you will predecease them, and when the opposite happens there is no comfort. Even the passing of all these years has done little to bring the peace I had hoped would eventually come my way. At long last I have been forced to face the inevitable - that it is an ache that will follow me to the grave.

And yet the intervening years have been wonderful to us, thanks mostly to our remaining three children. Again our lives took an upward swing and we have been blessed with many good years. This time they were marred only by the deaths of my mother and Bob's father within a month of each other. However, they were both in their mid-eighties and were beginning to hurt. Sad as we were to lose them, we were grateful they went quickly, sparing them the indignities of long and debilitating illnesses.

Our children have made us so proud. Brian, now a graduate engineer, reached his career goal at the young age of thirty-five when he was named plant manager of a large international company in Syracuse, New York. He and his wife Sherry gave us our first little treasure, our granddaughter, Kindra. Happily he has advanced even further in his career and is now program director of another international plant in Sherry's hometown of Burlington, Vermont. They are now hours closer and we can see them even more often.

Larry, with a degree in business, is a certified insurance counselor with a large firm not far from our home in Peabody. He married a girl from our parish and he and Michele had a home built in the town of Methuen, about twenty miles away from us, and not far from my family in Lowell. They gave us our three precious grandsons - Russell, Jeremy, and Nathaniel. We see them often and their visits are the highlight of our week.

Jane has kept us hopping more than anyone. Always a top student (her marks never faltered during our years of hell), she graduated near the top of her class and was accepted at all the best colleges, including two ivy leagues, Harvard and the University of Pennsylvania. She was offered a full scholarship to a midwestern university, but we knew she had her heart set on PENN, even preferring that over Harvard, so we sent her there and she had a wonderful four years.

Shortly after Bobby's death she took up the competitive sport of fencing. Joe Pechinsky, a Peabody fireman now retired, has been coaching fencers since the sixties. He had five Olympians and Jane came close to being his sixth. One night my friend Theresa Hynes called and said she wanted to get her daughter Janice into something different. She heard they gave fencing lessons at a local school and asked if Jane would also be interested in the sport. Would she! She said she always wanted to fence. That surprised me until she explained that after we saw "SWASHBUCKLER" at Radio City Music Hall she came home and got some sticks to show her friends how to fence. It was a sport she said she always wanted to try.

She and Janice were natural athletes and Joe was quick to realize their potential. He started giving them private lessons and put them into competition almost immediately. If the gym was closed, they would have their lessons between the fire trucks of the oldest firehouse in town.

Soon both girls were winning their share of medals. For the next ten years our families criss-crossed the country as we followed the girls from meet to meet. We met people from all over the country, renewing our friendships at each major competition. It was just the diversion we needed to get our minds off our loss of Bobby.

At fifteen Jane became a national champion by winning the Under-16 Junior Olympics in Tampa, Florida. She also made the finals of the Under-20, which surprised all of us.

At PENN she was put on the varsity team immediately and had an incredible freshman year, earning a spot on the junior national team, making her first trip to a competition in Europe. At the end of the year she earned first-team All America by placing third in the country at the NCAAs. She also helped her team to win the gold, the first time in the history of PENN that a women's team of any sport won the NCAA gold. Needless to say, her coach was elated. She made All America for two more years, falling out in her sophomore year when she was forced to fence with a hand cast. She also made All Ivy for all four years.

Her greatest delight was when she won the Junior Pan American gold medal in Mexico when she was nineteen, defeating all the other junior fencers in this hemisphere. It was a thrilling moment standing on the platform with the US flag being raised and the audience singing the national anthem. To her it was almost as good as winning the Olympics. We know Bobby was right up there on the platform with her.

As a result of her accomplishments, the Philadelphia Sports Writers Association honored her at their annual dinner, along with such notables as Julius Irving, the basketball player, and Jim Abbot, the one-handed pitcher. It was a heady year for a freshman college student. Since that time she has gone on to be a member of the national fencing team for three years and was a member of the gold medal team when they won the Pan-American Games in Cuba.

She tried hard to make the Olympic team, but missed out by only one point at a European competition Had she won that bout, she would have been on the 1992 Olympic team fencing in Barcelona. She is now working in the medical field and is happily married to a wonderful engineer from this area, Jim Carter. They bought a home not far from us and we also see them often. They have now given us our beautiful granddaughter Elizabeth, and little Joseph. Jane and Jim are both fencers and continue working in the sport by teaching at Jane's first fencing club. Fencing will always play a big part in both their lives.

After all these years it seems Bob, Jane and Brian have faced our loss easier than Larry and I did. Perhaps it was because I was his mother that I took it the hardest. In Larry's case I think it was the age of eighteen. He was the age I was when my father left us, and I had nightmares for years after he died.

Jane, at the age of eleven, did very well when Bobby died. However, when she was eighteen and lost my mother a week after starting college, she found it difficult to accept. I think it is that age when we are between youth and adult that losing a loved one is so difficult to face.

CHAPTER 27

Although we could have had a lawsuit against the automobile dealer and the garage, we thought it would be ludicrous to get rich off the death of our son. We didn't need their money, we needed our son, and all the money in the world wasn't going to bring him back to us. My mother always warned us that "blood money" never brought happiness. She was heartbroken when she watched two of her brothers split after the death of their father and they never spoke again for the rest of their lives. However, in hindsight, I wish we had at least held out for a high school scholarship in his name. It would have been the least they could have done, and Bobby certainly deserved it. It would also have given me a better feeling about the people at the garage.

Shortly after Bobby's death a new acquaintance, upon hearing his story for the first time, startled me when she asked if I had "gotten mad" at God for taking Bobby. In all honesty I had to reply, "No". For some strange reason she seemed to take umbrage with my answer. I could think of a dozen people I could have gladly strangled during those difficult years, but I couldn't get mad at God. He had given me so much in life.

I had a husband and children anyone would be proud to call her own. From the first time I went out with Bob I knew he would be dependable, but until our tragedy I didn't know just how strong he could be. In a situation where most men have been known to fall apart while the women seemed to become incredibly strong (or so we were told by personnel at both hospitals), Bob was incredible. Soft-spoken and easygoing by nature, he seemed to have a backbone of solid steel when things were at their lowest. He was ready to take on anyone who was a threat to Bobby, and often did. His quiet strength sustained all of us during those long and difficult months and I fail to see how the rest of us could have survived intact without him.

And he kept his troubles to himself. New acquaintances never heard about them until it was mentioned by someone else, and then they came forward and offered their condolences. Yet we all knew what a toll it was taking on him. Bobby was our firstborn and his namesake, the one for whom we had so many plans. Bob aged ten years in those twenty-five months, as did I. You can't live through a tragedy like that and come through unscathed.

I also had been blessed in my youth. Although I only had my father for eighteen years, I wouldn't have traded him for a lifetime with any other father. The deep faith and strong moral values he and Mother instilled in us has lasted me to this day. Those are the values we tried to instill in our own children. He was a strict father, but was a lot of fun. Long before swing sets became fashionable he built them in our yard, along with a see-saw, merry-go-round, sandbox, and other fun things to play with. Although we had one of the smallest yards in the neighborhood, our yard was where all the kids congregated because their own yards were so empty.

Mother didn't work outside the home so she was always there when we needed her. She made our clothes, uniforms for our cadet troop, and costumes for our plays. Like my father, she was strict, but oh so loving, and although we had the normal arguments most siblings have, all five children were very close - and are to this day. Sometimes there was a shortage of money, but never, ever, was there a shortage of love.

I could so easily have been in the position of that wonderful Pauline who cheered all of us up at the hospital. After her Billy was hurt, she and her husband split up and she was left to carry the burden alone.

Bad as our troubles were, they paled compared to a wonderful young couple who lived in back of us in Somerville. Behind our garage was a big cliff, so I didn't get to see much of the neighbors on the other street. This couple, however, happened to be friendly with another friend of mine, and it was through her that I heard their story.

Those parents had three sons the same ages as our three boys, and they all made their first communions together. I don't think there was a dry eye in the church as we watched them march up the aisle with their children in wheelchairs. All three boys had muscular dystrophy and the parents knew from birth that they wouldn't have them beyond their teens, and they didn't. Unlike them, we were able to enjoy Bobby's brief youth, always believing he would be with us until the day we died.

I also knew of several families who had perfectly healthy children killed in accidents, while at home they had a mentally retarded child, or a child who was having other problems. I guess as sorry as we feel for ourselves at the time, there is always someone worse off than we are.

CHAPTER 28

We believe in miracles!! We received two of them - albeit not the one we wanted, but miracles nevertheless. They are being included in this book, not because we expect others to believe in them, but because of what they meant to us - that God was right in the room with Bobby in Stoughton.

Shortly after the accident a postal employee, who worked downstairs from Bob's office, stopped Bob on the street to inquire about Bobby. He was only a casual acquaintance, so Bob was amazed when he opened his car door and took out a beautiful statue of the Sacred Heart of Jesus. It was on a high glass pedestal, surrounded by flowers, and had a tube going up in the middle with a fiberglass "waterfall" falling out of the top and cascading over the statue. Bob knew it must have cost him a sizeable chunk out of his pay check and was very surprised and grateful for his kindness.

We brought the statue to the hospital and set it on the dresser in Bobby's room. They were evidently afraid it would get knocked off and broken so they ordered a corner shelf to be built high above the bed, and there the statue remained until his death.

The day after the funeral Jim, the fellow who gave us the statue, called to apologize for missing the wake. With the holiday, many people didn't read the paper and didn't know about it until after the funeral. When Bob hung up from talking to Jim, Brian said he had something to tell us. He said when Joe Molino came to the funeral he mentioned that something odd had happened to the statue down at the hospital. Evidently everyone else down there knew about it except the Molinos and us. They knew if they mentioned it to Ann or Joe they would, in turn, tell us. Curious, I wrote to the nurse who was mentioned and the following letter was her reply:

December 29, 1978

Dear Mrs. Hall:
I received your letter through Mrs. Molino, and how I wish there were something I could say to help you feel better. I will relay the best I can what happened with Bobby's statue. It was something I did not mention at the time as I felt you were going through enough agony and I was unsure of how you would interpret it, as a sign of despair or a hopeful sign that could end in more disappointment. For this reason, I felt it was best to keep it to myself.
As best I can remember, it happened last spring. Bobby had been sitting up in bed with his

118

bedside table in front of him and his statue on the tray in such a way that they were facing each other. I had never seen him set up with his table in this manner before and it surprised me. I was planning to bathe him and do his treatments so I removed the statue and placed it on that high shelf to the right of his bed. I remember looking at the statue at that time, and there was nothing unusual - not being Catholic, I always have had a curiosity about what made a plastic statue so special, and for that reason I remember clearly looking at the statue and thinking those thoughts as I placed it on the shelf. There was no tear at that time.

I was called out of the room briefly and returned, filled his bath basin, gathered dressing supplies, and began to bathe Bobby. I was set up on the opposite side of the bed as the statue and the statue was quite high so I was sure I could not have splashed it accidentally.

While doing Bobby's care, I glanced at the statue and noticed a tear on the right cheek of the statue. I tried to think of every possibility of a definite cause for the water being on the cheek, but could not. I called Sterling because I felt if I told anyone later they would think I was seeing things.

This all occurred at about four o'clock in the afternoon. At ten o'clock the tear was still there - I was surprised it hadn't evaporated or rolled down in all that time. I looked closer and decided it had to be a plastic tear drawn on for effect, so I touched it - it was real and smudged on his cheek. The smudge also remained until I went home. It was gone the next time I worked and nothing unusual ever happened again.

As for Bobby's condition at the time, he was recuperating from a bout of pneumonia. He had a subclavian lead in and was receiving antibiotics, but he had already passed the worst point of the infection. Within a few days the course of antibiotics was finished and his IVs were discontinued.

Whether there is some message here, I do not know. I thought about it very much at first, but could not come up with any explanations. I guess there are things that happen to us all the time that there is no logical explanation for, and I decided I would just accept it as having happened and not worry about interpretations.

I know that you had great faith and I hope that you find comfort in knowing Bobby's suffering is over and he is at peace with God. I hope your own painful memories of Bobby's tragedy will ease and happier memories of better days shared with Bobby will take their place. Sincerely, Linda C.,

The other "miracle" concerned Bobby's cemetery plot. In recent years when our friends mentioned buying their cemetery plots I always said, "I love real estate, but that is one piece of real estate I'm not going to buy until I need it." When Bobby died I was so relieved to have him going in with my father.

The first Memorial Day after Bobby's death was coming up and Bob said he wanted something on his grave to signify he was there. I have a hard time with the cemetery, so he met Brian after classes one day and went to the cemetery. They would not allow a second stone on the grave, even though there was room for six people. Bob asked if they had any other land in that area that he could purchase, but they told him it had been sold out over thirty years earlier. He asked if there were any other plots in the cemetery, but was informed that it was all full and their annex was in an adjoining town, four miles away.

When they went back to the office and looked over the plot plan, one of the employees remembered a tree had been taken down a few months earlier, right near where Bobby was interred. Bob found out that the land was available and bought it immediately. Incredibly, it was just three gravesites away from where he was buried.

We bought a headstone the same size and color as my father's and had Bobby's name engraved on it, with a picture of the Sacred Heart of Jesus engraved on the front of the stone.

Bobby remained next to my father until the time of my mother's death. At that time we had him moved to his own gravesite, where he will be with us forever. Having that land become available after thirty years was, to us, our second miracle.

CHAPTER 29

Bobby must have been destined to be crushed to death from the beginning because he had two near misses, and the third one was fatal. In the summer of 1976 he had a day off and decided to work on his boat. It had a little leak and he was determined to find where it was.

Brian was working that day and Jane, Larry and I went up to Lowell to visit Mother. When we got home, Bobby looked a little pale, but didn't say anything to me. After supper Bob said he was taking him to the hospital. That afternoon, when he was alone, he had put some water into the boat to see where the leak was. Then he climbed underneath to see if he could spot it. The weight of the water caused the boat to shift and it ended up pinning him to the ground. He shouted, but no one was near enough to hear him.

Just as he was about to pass out, a woman down the street heard a faint cry and asked her husband to investigate. He found Bobby and leaned on the front of the boat to raise it off him. It ended up with him having three broken ribs. He was really hurting for over a week. It worried him and he kept saying, "Mother, I thought I was going to die."

A week or two before the accident at the garage, he and Pat were in New Hampshire for the day. Coming home at night, along the dark highway, he had a flat tire. It was the first one on his new car, and when he put the jack on it collapsed. He jumped out of the way just before he would have been pinned against the guard rail.

Fortunately he found a walkie-talkie in his trunk and was able to contact a fellow nearby who, in turn, called the police. The police kept the lights on while Bobby changed the tire with the jack furnished by the man on the walkie-talkie. That, too, scared him. Then, a short time later, he was really crushed, causing his death.

Much as we tried to keep him with us, and sorry as we are to have lost him, we now know in our hearts our prayers were answered - not the way we wanted them answered, but answered nevertheless.

We never prayed Bobby would just wake up. Rather, we prayed he would be returned to us "just the way he used to be", and when that wasn't possible he was taken. Knowing his proud and independent spirit, we know he would have been miserable coming back less than what he was. It would have been his own private hell on earth, and we know he deserved better than that.

When I see other coma patients who have come out of it and are disabled and unhappy, I know we wouldn't want that for Bobby. Now we can remember him as our handsome, healthy, twenty-one year old son. He will always be young to us.

CHAPTER 30

Looking back on it now, it surprises me that we came out of it as well as we did. I guess I had a wonderful example to follow in the courage of my mother. She is a story in herself. Widowed at forty-eight, she was left with a young family to raise. Although my father had been a fireman for over thirty-five years, most of them as a captain, when he died his pension died with him. Mother couldn't even receive Social Security because the firemen weren't covered by that, either. It was, indeed, a black time in our lives. I had just graduated from high school and my younger sisters were nine and twelve.

Mother was never one to sit down and feel sorry for herself. She decided she was going to start her own business. The man across the street had recently closed his store after eighteen years in business, so she decided to open one up in our living room. She had always been a homebody, never a club woman, and the thought of her facing the public surprised us, but we didn't voice our concerns.

During those eighteen years the neighborhood had been changed to "residential", but the other store was covered by the grandfather clause. We had to get petitions from the neighbors, which wasn't any trouble, but the planning board kept putting us off. Finally they gave us a permit on the first of March 1949. Mother thought it would be good luck to open the store on St. Patrick's Day - seventeen days to change a living room into a store. Thanks to my brother Fred, it was accomplished. We both worked during the day, but at night Fred would start building the shelves while Mother and I followed him around with paintbrushes.

Open it she did, on March 17, 1949, complete with green balloons and flowers all over the place. Fred gave her a green orchid and green carnations and he continued the tradition for the rest of her life.

When she was sixty-one years old, at a time when most of us are ready to retire, she took in her sister's three teen-aged children after her sister and husband died within five weeks of each other. She added two rooms onto her house to accommodate her new family. After all of us were married and she had the large house to herself, she rented the upstairs rooms and bath to college boys. They were still there at the time of her death. In the intervening years her business had gone downhill with the emergence of the large supermarkets and with many more cars available, so the added income from the college boys certainly was a blessing. More than that, however, was the fact that we felt safer having others in the house with her.

Mother operated that store until the age of eighty-six, at which time we converted it back into a living room. She enjoyed one happy year of retirement and died of a heart attack two days after our first grandchild was born, spending just one night of her life in the hospital. Mother was a very smart woman who read everything she got her hands on and retained everything she read. She traveled quite a bit and was enthusiastic about everything she saw. Her one fear was that her memory would fail her before she died. Gratefully it didn't; she was sharp until the day of her death.

My father had a large funeral because he was well known as a fireman, and Mother always said not many would come to her funeral. Quite the opposite was true - they were standing in line for an hour at her wake. She knew everyone in the neighborhood from operating the store, and the children thought a lot of her. Once, we came home from an afternoon off and she found balloons and a note from a couple of little girls who had been on vacation and had come back to visit her. It was such a cute gesture - and there were more.

Our family has many get-togethers and Mother was always the center of attention. At the time of her death she had five children, eighteen grandchildren and nineteen great-grandchildren, and she was close to them all. I'm happy our children had so many opportunities to enjoy her, as she spent all her vacations with us in New Hampshire, and was here at our home every week.

Jane wrote and delivered the following eulogy to her grandmother, which she wrote en route to the funeral.

Thank you for coming today and for letting me get up to say a few words about our beloved grandmother. We have come to say goodbye to a wonderful and remarkable woman. Whether she was called 'Mother', 'Nana', 'Great-Nana', 'Sister', 'Aunt' or 'Friend', she meant the world to all of us.

Nana was a special person who had faced many hardships in her life, but she stuck it out through all of them and was blessed with a large family. From the first child to the last great-grandchild she cherished each one of us and had a special place in her heart for all of us.

As a child I remember Nana as a woman who loved to have us at her house. Each week we would go into the store and pick out our penny candy. She could spoil us like any other grandmother, but she wasn't just any grandmother, she was our Nana.

Nana loved to watch her grandchildren grow. She had her hopes and dreams for all of us, and I don't think any of us ever let her down. When little Billy was born, no one could have been prouder than Great-Nana. Her great-grandchildren gave her new life as each one came along. She even knew her latest great-grandchild was a healthy girl.

Her son and daughters worshipped her. Just by looking at Nana one can see a remarkable woman who deserved all the respect she received. She was always there when her children needed her. She raised her children alone after God gave her a terrible cross to bear. One can only admire her courage and determination.

We are sad here today, but we can all think that Nana is standing next to Grampa looking down on us and she is saying, "Look at what we helped to conceive." And she is smiling!

Friends told me there wasn't a dry eye in the church, which was full, when she finished. Much as we now miss her, we are grateful she had such a peaceful death and is now happy in heaven with my father.

PATRICIA HALEY HALL

CHAPTER 31

Bob and I have been involved in every aspect of the children's lives. Because I didn't work during their formative years, I was with them constantly. However, I was born with a guilty conscience and after they were all married I wondered if I had been too strict, too bossy, if they would refer to me as "the witch". I needn't have worried. Recently I received a letter from Brian that put my mind to ease. It is a letter I will treasure forever. It went like this:

THE GIFT

It all started at the beginning. God made us in His image, and through His son showed us His love. And since that time generation to generation have learned from His word and passed His love on to their children.

The older and hopefully wiser I get, the more I realize how much my parents have given to me. Not only did they bring me into this world and shelter me during my fragile years, but they did much, much more. First, through their love and actions they taught me the meaning of real love for God and each other. They also taught me to believe in myself and gave me the freedom to grow and spread my wings as I became ready. My parents did all this out of constant love for me, even though when I was young I often did not see it that way. The constant discipline they used often met with resistance from me as I was growing up. But through all this my parents were always there when I needed them. For that I am eternally grateful to them and to God for giving me such good parents and great role models.

I recently read a quotation I believe was from Mark Twain that really hit home to me. As I remember it went like this: "When I was 18 my parents didn't really know anything, but as I get older they sure are getting smarter." I believe what he was saying is that when we are young we think we know it all and only when we get older and wiser do we realize how smart our parents really are.

I sometimes have a hard time adequately expressing my feelings and my love to you, Mother and Father, but I want you to know how lucky I feel to have had such wonderful, caring and loving parents. My only hope in life is that I can live up to the example you have set for me and pass the knowledge, love and guidance you have given me on to Kindra. I know it hasn't always been easy bringing me up, but I want you to know that as I get older and wiser I realize now what a superb job you have done."

Love, Brian

PATRICIA HALEY HALL

CHAPTER 32

Now that my book is finished, I am trying to concentrate more on the happy times we had with Bobby when he was alive, rather than the traumatic time we had with his illness and the sad times since he left us. We feel fortunate the years we had with him were so happy, and he was a son who made us very proud.

During all these years since Bobby's death I had tried over and over again to type my notes, but each time I transcribed a page the whole miserable affair came back and I had to put it aside for awhile. Somehow it was worse living through it the second time than it was the first, because then we had hope and now we knew the hopeless outcome. Now it is such a feeling of relief to have it out of my head and down on paper.

There are several reasons I wanted Bobby's story to be told, even if only the members of the family read it. I wanted him to be more than just a statistic - born in 1955 and died in 1978. To us he was so much more than that. Somewhere on record I wanted it known what he was and what he meant to us, how much we loved him and how sorely we now miss him. I wanted him to be a real person to our grandchildren and not just a name on a remote gravestone. I also hoped word would get back to the people at the garage and they would realize the heartache they had caused us, and how their callous dismissal of his death hurt almost as much as the death itself.

But even more than that, I'd like to think this book would do some good. Somewhere along the line I'd like to believe that hospital personnel, entrusted with the care of comatose patients, would read Bobby's story and get a little insight into what it is like for the families of those unfortunate victims. If it helps just one of them to be a little kinder, a little more compassionate, all my work will not have been in vain.

Larry has continued to talk about Bobby often over the years, always about the pleasant and funny things that happened when they were together. Recently we were on Lake Champlain in Vermont on Brian's boat when he started talking about some of the funny incidents that had happened when they were on our boat, and it left us all laughing. As a result, his children know of the uncle they never got to meet.

One night Larry called to say that he didn't want anything for Christmas because he had already received the best Christmas gift he could ever ask for. The teacher had asked his seven year old Russell what he would want for Christmas if he could have anything in the world he wanted. He surprised all of us by saying he'd want his Uncle Bobby to come back down from heaven. We knew then he would never be forgotten, that we would always have our own special guardian angel up in heaven looking down on us - our beloved Bobby.

TO ALL PARENTS

*"I'll lend you, for a little while, a child of mine,
He said,
For you to love while he lives, and mourn when
he is dead.
It may be six or seven years, or twenty-two or
three,
But will you, 'til I call him back, take care of him
for me?
He'll bring his charms to gladden you, and shall
his stay be brief
You'll have his lovely memories as solace for
your grief.
I cannot promise he will stay, as all from earth
return,
But there are lessons taught down there I want
this child to learn
I've looked the wide world over in my search for
teachers true
And from the throngs that crowd life's lanes, I
have selected you.
Now will you give him all your love - not think
the labor vain,
Nor hate me when I come to call to take him
back again.*

I fancied that I heard them say, 'Dear Lord, thy will be done.

For all the joy this child shall bring, the risk of grief we'll run.

We'll shower him with tenderness and love him while we may.

And for the happiness we've known, forever grateful stay.

And should the angels call for him much sooner than we planned

We'll brave the bitter grief that comes, and try to understand."

AUTHOR UNKNOWN